The Roller Coaster Decade

Order this book online at www.trafford.com/07-2525
or email orders@trafford.com

Most Trafford titles are also available at major online book retailers.

Edited by: Shiree Woolnough
Cover Designer: Shiree Woolnough
Back Cover copyright: Irene Moser-Spring

Note for Librarians: A cataloguing record for this book is available from Library and Archives Canada at www.collectionscanada.ca/amicus/index-e.html

ISBN: 978-1-4251-5634-3

We at Trafford believe that it is the responsibility of us all, as both individuals and corporations, to make choices that are environmentally and socially sound. You, in turn, are supporting this responsible conduct each time you purchase a Trafford book, or make use of our publishing services. To find out how you are helping, please visit www.trafford.com/responsiblepublishing.html

Our mission is to efficiently provide the world's finest, most comprehensive book publishing service, enabling every author to experience success. To find out how to publish your book, your way, and have it available worldwide, visit us online at www.trafford.com/10510

www.trafford.com

North America & international
toll-free: 1 888 232 4444 (USA & Canada)
phone: 250 383 6864 • fax: 250 383 6804 • email: info@trafford.com

The United Kingdom & Europe
phone: +44 (0)1865 722 113 • local rate: 0845 230 9601
facsimile: +44 (0)1865 722 868 • email: info.uk@trafford.com

10 9 8 7 6 5 4

A Hard to Believe True Story

Livia Moser

"We want a few mad people now.
See where the sane ones have landed us!"

George Bernard Shaw

"Experience is, for me, the highest authority.
The touchstone of validity is my own experience.
No other person's ideas, and none of my own ideas,
are as authoritative as my experience.
It is to experience that I must return again and again,
to discover a closer approximation to truth
as it is in the process of becoming in me.
Neither the Bible nor the prophets —
neither Freud nor research —
neither the revelations of God nor man —
can take precedence over my own direct experience.
My experience is not authoritative because it is infallible.
It is the basis of authority
because it can always be checked in new primary ways.
In this way its frequent error or fallibility
is always open to correction."

Dr. Carl Rogers

"The human being is under pressure
and was always under pressure until his very last breath."

Jakob Moser

"Madness is the best friend of courage;
sanity is the best friend of fear.
Choose your friends wisely."

Livia Moser

"In the face of adversity, laugh."

Livia Moser

"Geniuses have a different sense of what is real."

Michael Campbell

I dedicate this book to _______________(your name), because you either make a positive or negative difference in someone's life. Only negative influence can push others to rise to the occasion, so I suggest you stop wasting your energy being negative, because you are only depleting your energy and helping others realize their full potential.

This book is for all the sick people of Switzerland, don't remain a secret and keep fighting against those who want to keep you sick. Without you a large part of the Swiss economy couldn't work.

LIVIA MOSER

Funny, lazy and caring

Some Avenue
1200 Geneva
022 123 4567
tallulahbelle@xxx.com

NATIONALITY: Swiss
DATE OF BIRTH: 13.05.1976
STAR SIGN: Taurus
CHINESE SIGN: Dragon
PLACE OF BIRTH: Trinidad and Tobago

HOSPITAL STAYS: 1994–2004

State Hospital of Graubünden:
Kidney Biopsy

Mental Facility of Münsingen:
4 Months for schizophrenia

State Hospital of Geneva:
2 stays for thrombosis, 16 months of Dialysis, 3 weeks for kidney transplant, 2 stays for bipolar disorder, and 2 stays for kidney infection

Métarie Clinic:
One stay for bipolar disorder

State Hospital in Bern (Day clinic)
6 months for rehabilitation for mental illness

** Not in chronological order and all in Switzerland*

PILLS

Kidney:	Prograf, Cellcept, Atacand, Selipran, Folic Acid, Norvasc
To keep me sane:	Rivotril, Depakine

In other words I take a lot of pills everyday.

COUNTRIES LIVED IN

Birth–end of 1976	Trinidad and Tobago
1976–1980	Panama
1986–1986	Sri-Lanka
1986–1989	Thailand
1989–1993	Switzerland
1993–1994	Pakistan
1994–Present	Switzerland

LANGUAGES

German:	Supposed to be my mother tongue
English:	Mother tongue (unofficial)
French:	Fluent
Spanish:	Enough to get laid
Italian:	Enough to make people believe that I speak Italian

COMPUTER KNOWLEDGE

Microsoft Office:	(Word, Excel): GOOD
Internet:	VERY VERY EXCELLENT
Google skills:	Detective level

HOBBIES
Drama, talking in cafés, watching movies on the DVD and taking naps on the couch

Yes, my C.V. of being hospitalised is really impressive, but I would prefer if it never happened. To get through all of this I used my seventh sense and that is the under- glorified SENSE OF HUMOUR!!!! So I welcome you all to my roller coaster decade. Buy your ticket and ride with me through the past ten years.

Table of Contents

1

Summer of Magical Soap Bubbles

The Year 1994

> "In the book of life every page has two sides:
> we human beings fill the upper side
> with our plans, hopes and wishes,
> but providence writes on the other side,
> and what it ordains is seldom our goal."
>
> —*Nisami*

I stepped out of the airport into the warm sunshine of Switzerland. I was so relieved to be back in Switzerland. Not because I loved the country so much, but because I had a tough year behind me.

When I lived in Switzerland, I didn't realize all the things that I had had. Only while living in Pakistan, did I value the freedom that I had in Switzerland. All the things that I had taken for granted before, I cherished now, like the simple act of using public transport.

Spending my senior year in Pakistan was like a roller coaster ride through hell. I used to go to the International School of Bern for four years. I had to change to Pakistan for my senior year, because my father was transferred there with the company he worked for. I was in no mood to move there for not even a year. But in the end I had to go.

At the beginning of the year, I was trying to be positive about my 'not chosen' situation. Pakistan was a culture shock for me and I remember the night when I realized the vast difference between the cultures. It was at a private party and I can still remember the lyrics of the song *"My my my love is like bla bla tease tease me till I lose control."* Everyone was dancing and getting jiggy with it when the 23:00 prayer came on and one guy jumped up and stopped the radio. Absolute silence followed, everyone was seated and I stood there like an absolute idiot thinking which planet I had landed on. As soon as the prayer was over, everyone was back dancing to the same song like nothing had happened. That I still remember this night so vividly is confirmation to me that it was absolute madness and absolute hypocrisy.

The positivity of trying to adapt failed. It collapsed finally in October 93; I was again at a private party, not enjoying myself, but trying to talk about something, anything. I never experienced this kind of loss of words before. Every time I tried to talk, one or two words would come out and then I would retreat into silence again. I was racking my brain for something to say, but my whole vocabulary was deleted. I guess my computer crashed because of some unknown virus. Blocked and confused to what was happening to me I remained silent and was relieved when the party ended.

That evening silence draped my lively personality like a sheet on a corpse and I fell into a depression so deep, all I wanted to do was hide in the closet. And a couple of times later I did. My mother found me in the closet, staring into space. She asked me what was wrong, but all I could say was nothing. The truth was nothing that I could place my finger on was wrong. If only I knew, I could have solved it. My depression was so bad I quit smoking. Now that is campaign slogan right there for the anti smoking lobbyists, "Get depressed and you'll give up smoking."

That talkative, lively personality that was Livia was replaced by a disco ball with no lights shining on it. I tried really hard to find my personality but it was gone and all I felt was complete numbness. I no longer cared what happened to me.

My hair started falling out and a colony of zits invaded my back. When I looked in the mirror I saw a strange girl with no light in her brown eyes. I told her that she would never amount to anything, because she was stupid and worthless. She would never be loved so she might as well give up now.

For the months following that night I was a zombie, trying hard to recapture my former personality, because I missed my former personality so much. I should have put an ad in the newspaper, "Have you seen a personality with no body attached? Please contact Livia at the following number." Since there was no dazzle in me, people forgot about me to find a new piece of action. I mean, would you hang around a jukebox that didn't work???

My personality crashed back like a meteor one day in February 94 and I was back and even stronger. I was myself again and enjoying life. The whole high school noticed that I was happy again and that Livia was back.

Soon dirty rumours spread around like wildfire and I even had the honour of my name spray painted all over the wall. It wasn't a declaration of love that was for sure. What was written instead was, "Livia is a free fuck," with red spray paint on a white wall (The colours of Switzerland). The weird thing about this 'flattering' writing on the wall was that it was on the only day my mother drove my sister, Carmen and I to school, because the driver couldn't drive us. It is as if the Picassos in Lahore knew in advance she was driving us.

I didn't really care and I almost found it funny, but my mother's reaction was one of fury. She parked the car, marched into school and bee lined straight to the principal's office. She told him that they remove it immediately. Whatever she told him worked, because it was gone after school.

Carmen's reaction was very different. She went into the bathroom and started crying. Someone came to tell me that my sister was crying in the bathroom. I ran to the bathroom and called out her name. "Why are you crying?" I asked, she said, "I don't understand how you can handle this; you don't deserve to be treated like this." I told her that these people weren't worth it and if I were upset they would have won.

The best thing about the rumour mill was that I didn't care. I had too much integrity to let a bunch of cowards with a perpetual identity crisis bring me down. I would have had more respect if one of those idiots would have stepped out of the shadows and told me straight to my face "You are a bitch". But no one ever did. The rumour mill may have stopped if I had cared, but since I didn't, the rumours became more and more outrageous. Once I was pregnant, another time I had an orgy with six men. It was so ridiculous. How could I possibly take it seriously?

The high school students were very lucky that my older sister Sarah wasn't there. She was studying in Canada. She would have beaten everyone up, because she would have never accepted that two of her sisters had been attacked. The image in my mind makes me laugh. Students lying around on the floor like half dead flies while Sarah continued to bulldoze her way to find anyone else who needed a lesson of respect.

There was one positive aspect to Pakistan and that happened in April when I got together with Ahmed. He was a nice guy with a car and he gave me a very precious gift, freedom in a country where it was scarce. To him I will always be grateful. Sadly a year later he died in a car crash. How ironic that a car which gave me freedom, killed him. But maybe he is now freer than I could ever dream of being.

On May 13th, 1994 I turned 18 and all hell broke loose. On my birthday my parents arranged a great party and the theme of the party was hippies and punks. I was upstairs tearing my jeans apart when my mother came up to get me, because guests were arriving. She saw me and ran out. I don't know what she had seen that night, but later she said that there was an evil look in my eyes and that she didn't recognize me anymore. She believed that a girl had slipped drugs in my drink.

The party was fun and I was oblivious to my mother's reaction, because I was having too much of a great time, but things definitely changed after that. I was getting more and more daring and reckless. That night I leaned out of a car at high speed. You can easily put it down to the fact that I was an omnipotent teenager, but it was not in my nature to be that reckless.

The past events were just the 'waiting in line' part to get on the roller coaster, but now I was really on it.

It was the beginning, the part where you are sitting and it's just moving, but this roller coaster was one which was invisible to me and to everyone else.

One day in May, a week before graduation, I went to a boy's bathroom to smoke a cigarette on school grounds and someone must have told the principal, because he caught me. I thought I was being smart, by going into the boy's room, because then everyone would think it was a guy who smoked. Yes I was an idiot. My intelligent tactic led me to expulsion from school and attendance to my high school graduation only with a signature from my parents that I would behave.

Now I would like to continue with my logic, because looking back it wasn't logical, but plain stupid. I went to Bangkok, Thailand, to visit my friend. I stole stationary (which I even had the money to pay for) from a department store and to be smart I thought I would stay there and have a drink in the café so the clerks wouldn't get suspicious. That is where they caught me. I immediately went to jail. The two nights I spent in the jail were the nights my friend was graduating. There is only one thing to say to this, IDIOT.

Jail wasn't as bad as you might think. The food was good, my inmates and I were like a family sharing cigarettes and I traded a ring for a Thai massage. I remember singing *"Country Roads"* to a blind man as he tapped along. The guards thought I was crazy.

Though I couldn't communicate with my inmates, because they were all Thai, I managed by signing and pointing. Laughing is also a universal language so that worked. Luckily my best friend's family gave me some magazines and didn't leave me there to rot.

I did, however, have ridiculous fantasies of a prince coming to save me, but why would a prince come to save me when I had put myself in this situation? It was pointless to even think like this. But it helped to let the time pass by.

The party ended when my mother showed up and saw her daughter behind bars. I then realized what an awful mistake I had made. I felt awful. Not only had I embarrassed myself, my family, but also my best friend's family. That my best friend forgave me is still a miracle. But she taught me an invaluable lesson about true friendship. It took me over a year to forgive myself.

My mother bailed me out. All I could do was cry and cry in the police station. I had no excuse and all I could say was that I was sorry. But that wasn't the end of the legal process. My mother called an old colleague of my father's in Bangkok and spoke to him. He managed to help with the Thai authorities. My mother also had a friend called Pia Thep who also helped. She had met him when we lived in Bangkok years back and by coincidence he also knew the department store owners. (Unfortunately he died years later, bless his soul).

I remember an evening when I met the owners and they were so nice to me that it made me feel even more awful. All I could think of was why were they being so nice to a petty thief. I have no idea what the owners did or said but I wasn't black listed from Thailand for five years and I wasn't going to be deported in hand cuffs to the Swissair flight out of the country.

We walked all over Bangkok those two weeks dealing with the authorities, because I still had to wait for the court case and the final verdict of the judge. All this for stationary, but stealing is still stealing and it was taken seriously in Thailand.

The court case was another fiasco, but it forced me to really open my eyes. After leaving jail, I had to go to court to see if the Thai judge would let me leave the country or make me do a term of 2 months in a Thai prison. I sure as hell didn't want to go to prison for 2 months, because the inmates in there would not be as nice. I am certain that if I sang *"Country Roads"* in a prison they probably would have cut my tongue off and shoved it somewhere where the sun definitely doesn't shine.

I went to court extremely nervous to hear the result of the verdict. My lawyer assured us that I would be free to go. As I sat in the courtroom with my mother and lawyer, I looked around me. I saw a candy store of scum. There were hookers, transvestites, thieves, criminals, gamblers and me. Educated, coming from a family that loved me and having everything within reason it dawned on me that I was no better than the rest of them.

The feeling of shame hit me like a truck. All I wanted to do was throw up. Then I realized that this was the fork in the road and that I had a choice. It was either go into the underworld or to survive honestly in the world. I chose my way and I chose to take the honest route. As soon as I made my choice in my mind I was taken out of the larger courtroom and taken into a smaller courtroom. There the judge let me go. I profusely thanked him. He then said that he had been much more lenient than the Swiss police. I was in no position to inform him that in Switzerland all they would have done is fine me 50. - CHF and call my parents for the same crime.

Finally we were on an airplane to Switzerland. My mother was obviously not too pleased with me. I could see it written all over her face as we sat in the train going to our final destination, a small town in Switzerland near Bern. My mother understandably was too angry to speak to me.

Since my mother didn't want to speak to me I looked out the window and saw through God's video camera what life was all really about. The weather changed very quickly. First there was rain, clouds, sunshine and even a rainbow. The weather was portraying what life really is. Clouds when you are down, sunshine when you are happy, rain when your life is just shit and rainbows in those extra special moments in a person's life. It was so beautiful and sad that it brought tears to my eyes.

As the train chugged away I was thinking how happy I was to have all the troubles and pain behind me. I could look forward to 2 months of summer vacation and then starting Hotel Management School. That was the plan since I was 12. It was my choice, actually the first choice that I alone made in my life.

As a young girl I loved hotels, the particular smell 5- star hotels had. My father told me that as a 2 year old I hung up a do not disturb sign on the door; of course I can't remember doing this. Living in Bangkok, Thailand, I had seen some beautiful hotels and every time I stepped into a hotel I felt immediately at home.

That was my dream; to one day have my own hotel. I already had my logo and everything. In my head I could walk through my hotel and see the happy staff and guests. It was going to be the happiest place on earth next to Disneyland. So yes you could say I had my whole life planned for me, but life had different plans in store for me.

The first person to greet us when we got off the train was my younger sister Carmen; she was happy to see us and relieved that I was still alive. She gave us a warm hug. She took us up to the apartment and my older sister; Sarah was there to greet us. There was also a stranger in the house; actually he was Sarah's friend from University. His name was Sava and he was a great cartoonist, especially when it came to drawing penises like comic figures. They weren't profane, just hilarious. We got along immediately.

Later I called my friends to see what they were up to and we were going to meet at the usual spot. They noticed I was more hyper than usual, but after living in a restricted society for 10 months, who wouldn't be. I apologized to my close friends for not being at their high school graduation, but that I had to go the court in Thailand.

My friends laughed about this whole episode, especially that I was so stupid, but I didn't mind, because I fully deserved it. The next day my friends and I went to a public pool next to the River Aare in the heart of Bern.

As I sat there in a bikini, a beautiful blonde man passed me. While he was walking past me, we held eye contact. I could see that he was pleased with what he saw from the bulge growing in his swimming trunks. My friends also noticed and we all had a good laugh.

Life was bliss and there were no worries in the world. All of us had graduated from high school, so we were still in that post graduation euphoria state. The state that comes before life will completely change for us all. We also knew that our little group would be split up across the globe. Catherine was going to England, Lisa to Sweden and Beatriz to Colombia. Only I would remain in Switzerland.

One afternoon Sarah asked me if I could replace

her at the café where she worked, because she wanted to work at the bank full time. I was glad to help her out and make some extra cash.

The next day she took me to the café. It was a small café with a huge terrace right next to the parliament and the drug scene. I thought that this was really ironic that these extreme worlds could be neighbours. But that is the beauty of Switzerland. I can't imagine people melting their drugs on spoons and injecting it into their veins next to the White House. This image made me laugh out loud. Yes, Switzerland was pretty liberal.

Sarah showed me all the tasks and how to use the cash register. It wasn't that complicated and soon enough I got the hang of it. I even made some tips. It was funny how old people gave me 20 Rappen as a tip and thought they were being overly generous. I wasn't complaining it was better than nothing. It seemed like it was going to be a regular summer job. But I was wrong.

On the second day on the job Sarah didn't come with me. I walked to the café and prepared my station. Then I met him...Bernard. He was also a waiter. With his dark brown hair and beautiful blue eyes he was quite a dish. What I noticed most about him was his aura. He radiated something almost magical. Soon enough I started talking to Bernard. He told me a little about himself and though we led two completely different lives we were on the same wave length and immediately clicked.

He had grown up on a farm in a tiny Swiss village. His parents had seven children. They didn't have enough money to travel, so he hadn't seen much of the world. His English wasn't very good. Because of my parents, I had travelled the world, went to International Schools and only had two sisters.

Bernard and I spoke Swiss German. I could see that he was really intelligent and though he never travelled he knew a lot about the world. He had his eyes wide open. Even though we came from two different worlds we found a common plateau that we could easily communicate on...Swiss German.

Bernard and I also really worked well together. We were able to communicate with our eyes. When I needed help, he would be there and vice versa. On the third day of work we went for a drink afterwards. We spoke for quite a while and then he invited me to his brother's apartment. I gladly went. I noticed he lived in Bern-Bethlehem. I never noticed that there was even a Bern-Bethlehem, so immediately I thought Bernard had something to do with God.

What impressed me most about the apartment was the queen-sized waterbed. Never one to hold my unbridled happiness back, I ran and jumped on the waterbed. He must have thought I was nuts, but I didn't care. After the waterbed jump, I saw a soccer ball and we played indoor apartment soccer. He was quite good at it. For a split second he reminded me of my Pakistani X-boyfriend (another one) who loved soccer with a passion. Could this be him in Bernard's body? Was he a soul traveller that followed me to Switzerland? I didn't think so! Where the hell could I come up with such a stupid idea? I put it down to some distorted romantic notion.

After playing soccer he showed me at least 36 pictures of his ex-girlfriend. Her name was Nelly and she worked in a mental hospital in Münsingen. I wasn't jealous, but I didn't really understand what he was trying to achieve by showing me pictures of her. So I registered it in my mind and left it there, somehow knowing that it would be useful. The mystery to me was that I didn't know what all this information of a strange woman would bring me.

Bernard was lying on the waterbed after the manual slide show when I strategically landed near him. I was dying to kiss him. When I landed near him, he looked at me and then we started kissing. It was the sweetest kiss I had ever experienced in my life. After the kiss we started talking about nothing and everything. I told him about my great grandmother who couldn't remember anything and he said that her brain is full of calcium residue like a washing machine. At the exact same time we burst into a jingle for a commercial that removes the calcium residue from washing machines. Our brains seemed connected. I felt like I had met my soul mate.

After so much talking and kissing we got so

hungry we ate a pizza. While we ate he spoke to me in French and it was so damn sexy that I wanted to jump him again. Unfortunately our afternoon ended, because I had to leave to meet my friend in town. He drove me into town. I gave him my phone number.

The next day on my way to work I bought a soap bubble maker. As I walked through the city I was blowing soap bubbles. Here I was 18 years old blowing bubbles like a kid. I didn't care how I seemed to appear to other people. I had always enjoyed blowing bubbles so why should I stop now. Since it was a sunny day the sunlight reflected off the bubbles making them beam in different colours. It was so beautiful and I was fascinated.

These bubbles represented those wonderful moments in my life, so magical, so overwhelming but never lasting and just as these bubbles popped so did those moments in my life. No matter how long I wanted to hold on to the moments I couldn't because they would go away just as these bubbles did in the July sun.

Up ahead I saw three construction workers slaving away in the heat, so I stopped bubble blowing. I went up to them and asked them if they wanted some water. They said, "Yes, please." I went to the nearest supermarket and bought 3 bottles of water. As I was about to pay I realized that I didn't have any money on me. Oh Shit! Out of nowhere a lady appeared and paid the drinks. I thought that this was strange, because in Switzerland a thing like this rarely happens. I took the bottles of water and passed them to the construction workers.

They were immensely pleased and wanted to pay me for the drinks. I told them it was free. Now they were even more shocked. It was probably the first time that someone offered them something free while they were working. It was also a new experience for me. I had never done this before in my life. I was never that generous, but more importantly, I would have never seen their thirst. Normally I would have walked right past them, not thinking twice if they wanted something to drink.

Something strange was happening to me, something great and unexplainable. It seemed every living part of me was alive. My senses were amplified and my awareness of the world and its inhabitants heightened. I was reaching a higher level of happiness and I loved every minute of it.

At work I noticed things I hadn't noticed before. Since it was Bernard's day off, he wasn't there to share it with me. First I saw a young man who seemed really sad. I went up to him and after serving his coffee I asked him what was wrong. He said that a job interview didn't go too well. I told him not to worry and that many other jobs would come along, so I offered him a croissant on the house. That seemed to make him feel a little bit better.

After I left him I went to serve another customer,

a couple with a shy child. She seemed so bored, so I handed my soap bubbles over to her. I showed her how to use it. At that moment my boss saw me and he wasn't pleased, but didn't say a word. But more important was that the child was happy.

There were some other boys from England and I could see that they had been travelling around Europe because of their backpacks. They knew I wasn't English, but I put on an English accent for the fun of it. They were pleased because I was making an effort. They ordered two sodas and I made a big lemon display. They were so happy to finally get some friendly service that they gave me a big tip. I told them that they needed it more than me. They refused to take the tip back.

The lemon cutter saw how many lemons I gave them and was angry with me. "I cut lemons all day and you use them like that, what are you crazy?" he said (What happened to the guest is king?) "Look I will buy you a lemon and cut it myself!" I replied. End of discussion. Also I didn't want his negative energy to ruin my happy state. I was enjoying my work. I played with children, fed the sparrows and served my guests with the utmost hospitality.

At lunchtime I couldn't eat my pork chop, so I put it in a bag and hid it behind my waitress purse, waiting for the right moment to give it away. I saw my chance when a drug addict walked by with a German shepherd. I knew that he didn't have much money, so I gave the pork chop to him to give to his dog. He was quite shocked, but gladly accepted it. Well that solves the pork chop problem.

I left work on a cloud; this was turning out to be a fantastic summer. I couldn't understand what was happening to me. I felt really powerful, like I was on top of the world and I also noticed that the magical events started speeding up.

In the train station of Bern I saw a young boy at one of the jewellery stands. He was staring at something with so much longing. I could hear his thoughts "If I only had the money, I could buy the ring". Taking immediate action I went up to him and asked him which ring it was? It was a ring with a marijuana leaf on it. O.K maybe it's not the best present to give to an 8-year-old boy. I bought the ring for him. When he finally had it in his hands he looked at me with amazement. I told him to take care and left, knowing that I would never see him again.

The next day at work I saw that there was a bouquet of flowers. I asked my female boss if I could use them, and she said yes. That very same day, one of the guests had a birthday so I gave her a flower. Another woman came with a beautiful sunflower. I asked her where she got it, because I love sunflowers and she said that it was from her garden. Bernard also noticed the sunflower and made remarks on it. Bernard had a special way with guests; he was kind and caring especially with old people.

An old woman came to the café everyday and drank four cups of coffee. Bernard was afraid that she would dehydrate so he always brought her a glass of water and cookies. He could sense she was lonely, so he even took the time to speak to her everyday. Yeah, Bernard was something special. He was one in a million and I was falling in love with him.

After work we went to see *"Four Weddings and a Funeral."* In the cinema I noticed a lot of girls were staring at him. He also noticed. I told him, "They probably think you are Hugh Grant", since he looked a lot like him. We had a good laugh.

During the movie there was one scene where they showed the wedding invitation for Bernard and Lydia. This was really freaky. Was there a message from this movie? Is Bernard my soul mate? Am I going to marry him? This freaked me out. I really believed that Bernard and I were going to get married. In my mind I saw the whole ceremony. It would take place at the café where we worked. Here I was imagining the wedding when I met this guy only a few days ago. To me everything made sense. He was really my soul mate and the events that happened would confirm it.

After leaving Bernard I got on the train. I sat in front of an old man with grey hair, well, what was left of it, and big blue eyes. He was reading something in a magazine. Then he started telling me what he was reading. It was about how much money it took to make *"Four Weddings and a Funeral."*

What a coincidence, I just came from watching this movie. I also noticed that this old man had the same blue eyes as and the same gestures as Bernard. Realization hit me. Bernard was a soul traveller who was in this man's body. I acted normally; it was sort of an unspoken agreement not to mention my enlightenment. This was also the reason I could never reach him on the phone; he was always following me. Wow I thought this was great. I never thought this could happen to me.

When I got home I lightened my hair, I sprayed the dye on my wet hair and blow-dried it. I was pleased with the results, not only was my hair a beautiful colour, but it also looked much healthier. As I stared at myself in the mirror, I realized that I had become more beautiful. My face had cleared up; I didn't have any of those zits that I had in Pakistan. Also the sun had given my skin a golden hue.

The transformation I was seeing in the mirror was amazing. Just 6 months ago in Pakistan I look liked a drug addict with thin hair, zits everywhere and my eyes were a dull brown. I felt like shit with zero confidence. But now, now I looked like some goddess. I was also becoming more and more beautiful with each passing day. As the feeling of euphoria grew in me so did my appearance. Everyday I was getting more powerful. The soap bubble wasn't bursting this time.

That night I went out. I had 45 minutes to kill before meeting my friends. I passed by the Bellevue

Palace, a 5 star hotel in Bern. As if a force was dragging me I went to the terrace. The terrace was beautiful and it had a splendid view of Bern and the mountains. I took a seat and ordered some wine. A lot of people seemed to be looking at me, maybe they too had noticed the glow that surrounded me or at least that was what I thought. It was probably because I was wearing shorts and a t-shirt, since I was so high I didn't notice.

I was enjoying my wine and the beautiful music coming from the shiny white piano. I approached the piano player, an old man with a very round face. He too had blue eyes. I asked him to play the song *"Memory"* from Cats, since it is one of my favourite songs. He said that he would play it only if I sang. So I sat next to him and sang.

Sitting next to him with the magnificent view and the beautiful tune, I experienced a sense of eternity. An enormous amount of inner peace enveloped me and I knew that the year 1994 would be a year of world peace. In my mind I thought that this man next to me was an angel; who was a messenger from God, telling me that God did really exist. I could feel his divine presence all around me. Everywhere I looked God was around. Knowing this I had nothing left to fear, inside me grew a courage, a courage so strong, so unshakeable and I never felt this brave before in my entire life.

When the song came to an end, I thanked him

and asked him what his name was and he said, "Dave, I am the only Swiss in Switzerland." I started laughing. Was he trying to tell me that the real Swiss people were a race who had a great joy of living; but Satan had put a curse over this blessed, beautiful land of peace to make them miserable? With this in mind I left the terrace. I had friends to meet.

I was sitting with my friends when I heard some music. I decided to check out the commotion with two other guys. It was a band playing some tunes. The band had just finished playing their music when we got there. I went up to the manager, standing by the stage. I asked him if I could sing three songs. He acted as if somehow he had been expecting me. How was that possible though? I got up on stage and sang *"Memory"*, *"Country Roads"* and *"The Greatest Love of All"*. I don't have a good voice, but all these songs were sung from the heart.

As I stood there on stage with no accompanying music, looking at the stars and feeling the magic that had entered my life I just wanted to cry. I got really emotional. For once in my life I felt I had come home, that finally I had roots somewhere and this home was the city of Bern. Bern had become an oasis, and I was the lost traveller who came to quench a thirst that I didn't even know I had.

After I finished people clapped and I got off the stage, returned to my friends and left. I would never have had the guts to sing in front of all those people before, but with my newfound courage I could do anything. There were no inhibitions left in me, the rules of society didn't apply to me anymore. Society was like an invisible monster that everyone feared. I no longer feared that monster. It could no longer tell me what to do. The only thing I listened to now was my instincts and my impulses. If my heart wanted me to do it, I would. I didn't care what anyone thought of me.

My friends thought I was crazy, they also thought I was high as a kite even though I wasn't taking any drugs. One friend told me that if I didn't relax I would end up hugging the Swiss cross on top of the parliament. We all had a good laugh. Yes it was another fun evening in Bern.

The next day I had a brilliant idea, I would bring my camera to work with me. I bought film and while I was working took pictures of the clientele. The pictures would be a collage of human nature. I started snapping away; luckily my boss didn't see me. I took pictures of an old man with his granddaughter, a couple in love, another couple in love, but hadn't yet expressed it, business people, young girls gossiping away, a bunch of boys getting a drink before they got on their bikes, an old woman feeding the sparrows and a drug addict concentrating on drinking her coffee. Then a colleague told me that the president of Switzerland was having a coffee at the far end table.

I immediately went up to him and asked him if

I could ask him just one question. He said, "Yes". I asked him "Why aren't the Swiss people happy?" He replied, "They have too much." I agreed and asked him if I could take a picture with him. He agreed and we took a picture together. His presence reminded me of my dead grandfather. My heart told me that my grandfather was in his body. I was convinced he had come down from heaven to see how I was doing. What another coincidence that I decided to take a picture on that particular day, it was just another example of how my life was controlled by a higher force.

After my shift, Bernard and I went to the swimming pool. Bernard moved positions and I saw a glimpse of his penis in the side of his trunks. A weird sensation went through me. It was so natural to see his penis. Of course I didn't mention it. I started singing *"Memory"*, Bernard just looked at me. His blue eyes became lighter and lighter.

While I was singing he seemed to be in a trance and there was a sign of recognition in his eyes, as if I had sung this song before, but that was impossible, I never sang this song to him. Except...no...unless he was in the body of the piano player at the Bellevue terrace. Bernard had once again followed me. Was it really him? These realities made my head spin. Who was this Bernard anyway? Was he some kind of alien who transformed into other people's bodies? Or was he God in a mortal body? Of course I didn't share my discovery with him. It was too earth shattering to speak about. Now it made sense why he took me to Bern-Bethlehem. We were going to eventually make love and have Jesus II.

I left Bernard and started walking towards the train station. My feet were really hurting because of the blisters I got from running around as a waitress. At that exact moment a man on a bicycle rode by and saw how much pain I was in. He offered me a ride to the train station; man was I grateful to him. When we got to the train station I thanked him for his unnecessary act of kindness.

I walked through the train station and saw the back of a guy who was helping an old man. I knew who it was. It was JESUS! I wanted to see his face. All I could see was his long brown hair, but just as quickly as he had come he had gone. Where was he? I just saw him. If Jesus was here it must be the year when the world will have world peace. He was here to save us all. I was out of breath, shit I just saw Jesus... WOW but I knew that I couldn't tell anyone, they would just think I was nuts. So I kept it to myself, but it made me smile.

I got on the train, back to the village where the rented flat was. I bought a postcard and wrote some inside jokes for Bernard. I went to the stamp dispenser and put my money in. It accepted the money, but didn't give me any stamps.

Then I suddenly remembered I had bought a stamp last week that I left in my wallet. It was a beautiful stamp. It had a big heart with a gold cross in the middle. On either side of the cross there was a sun and a moon. This was another message. Bernard was really my soul mate and he was God.

With a happy heart I returned to my flat. I just chilled out and watched some television. It was strange, but everything that came on television had some connection with me. I saw myself. Even the songs I heard meant something to me.

As I switched to MTV I saw the video *"Love is All Around"* by Wet Wet Wet. This song reminded me of Bernard and *"Four Weddings and a Funeral."* Even Wet Wet Wet meant something to me, because I was always wet around him, no actually one day I was drenched because I was speaking to Bernard when it was raining. That day I didn't care that it was raining. I enjoyed it, while my sister thought I was nuts. After I heard the song I knew it was a sign to call him. I called him and for the first time he was at home. But as usual he was too busy to see me so I stayed at home. Of course God has a lot of things to do.

Later that night I went to bed. I couldn't fall asleep, so my eyes wandered around the room. I spotted the silhouette of a man and a woman talking in the next window. It seemed a bit fuzzy, so I went up to the window and there was no one there. I went back to bed and there they were again. It was silver light that constructed these two figures, and then they started dancing and got on a carpet and took off into the dark night full of stars.

It finally dawned on me that I was having a hallucination. I wasn't even on drugs and I had not consumed any alcohol. Either I was going nuts or had seen way too many Disney movies. Figures don't just appear, start twirling and then take off on a carpet. I honestly didn't believe I was crazy and enjoyed every minute of this spectacular hallucination. It was an extraordinary miracle and I was lucky to be a part of it.

Just as I was falling asleep there was a procession of small angels walking towards me, another hallucination. Then I heard the most beautiful rendition of *"Memory"* in my head. It seemed like angels were singing to me.

That night I realized that there was so much more to this world than meets the eye. I had walked around the world with my eyes closed and took all that I saw as the ultimate reality. Compared to the world I was experiencing now with hallucinations, magical coincidences, soul travellers and the ever presence of God (even in the mortal body of Bernard), I mean even Jesus was in the picture, I had lived a reality that had been like seeing a silent black and white movie.

Now I was seeing the big picture, that everything connects and how my path had been set out for me. All I had to do was follow the signs that I couldn't see in the past. The only thing that I wasn't aware of was why was I experiencing all this? Was I supposed to be some kind of messenger who was supposed to shed some light on the magic of the world or awaken others from their sleep, because right now I saw magic everywhere and the potential of humanity?

When I woke up from the best sleep I ever had, the first thing I did was buy thirteen sunflowers and thirteen cards. On every card I wrote, "A person without a dream is like the sky without the sun." After attaching the cards to the sunflower, I headed straight to the drug scene of Bern and distributed them to the junkies.

After seeing the drug addicts, I saw that there was no hope left in them. With the sunflowers and cards, I wanted to give them the feeling that there was still hope left out there for them. I chose the sunflowers, because they open their heads to the warm rays of the sun and they follow the sun. Yellow is also the colour of hope.

After distributing the cards I took some photos of the drug scene. One of my favourite pictures was of a girl totally passed out with a sunflower in her hat. It was a picture of doom and gloom, side by side, two extremes that made a whole.

One drug addict came up to me and asked what the hell did I think I was doing and told me that it was forbidden to take photos. He was angry and he had every right to be. Then another drug addict, a girl whom I had previously helped get to the bathroom at the café where I worked, said it was all right. The man apologized to me. I told him that there was no need for an apology, because I was the one invading their privacy. The drug addicts were stupefied and didn't understand why this girl was passing out sunflowers, but they thanked me and told me I was a good girl.

I left the drug scene to start my shift at the café. Half way through work, I was called to the boss's office. He informed me that I was fired, because I didn't do my job properly. I was really upset, because I enjoyed working there. Nevertheless I didn't hang my head down, but bought chocolates and champagne. I was going to celebrate my being fired in style with my colleagues.

As I parted ways with my colleagues, I called my mother and told her the news, I was so angry I was crying. She told me to come home, so I did. The next day my parents and I were walking when I stopped with a scared look on my face.

My parents asked me what was wrong. I replied that I hated that man on the street walking five meters from us. They were stunned and I only found out about ten years later that there was no man, only I had seen him.

My parents thought there was something wrong with me, which was when the bubble burst. We were going to make a tour of the doctors in Bern. At first we all went to our own doctor, a doctor who specializes in tropical diseases; because during most of our expatriate lives we lived in tropical countries. He took blood and urine samples and tested them for drugs. No drugs were found. This first round I passed. Next I had to undergo a CAT scan. I felt like a big penis entering this huge electronic vagina. I had no tumours and nothing unusual happening in my brain. Yeah, I passed again.

Next I had to see a psychiatrist. She tested me with pictures that I remembered doing in kindergarten. It's where you put different colours of paint on a piece of paper, fold it and open it and you get patterns. Now I know it is called the Rorschach test. But hers were in cardboard probably taken from kindergarten children, reprinted and sold at an exorbitant price since it was a specialized test. She asked me what I saw on the overpriced cardboard pictures. I told her the obvious, that any idiot could see.

I felt victorious I had passed all three rounds. There was nothing wrong with me. But that was not enough, we went back to the tropical doctor and he gave me this huge injection with some kind of fluid, unknown to me. After that I was useless. My neck went into a two-day spasm. It turned almost all the way around. I must have looked like a retarded swan. I was also informed that I wasn't going to start Hotel Management School. That prick (both the needle and the doctor) from the injection destroyed the magical soap bubble.

Whatever I was taking gave me constant butterflies in my stomach. I couldn't sit; I couldn't stand, so the only way to calm down was to take

5 hot baths a day. I took refuge underwater. It was calm down there. I would also change clothes 5 times a day because I couldn't leave the apartment. One evening I went out the bedroom window, jumped on a garbage container and walked around. It was a beautiful night. But my family soon found me and put me back into the apartment.

I was under constant supervision; there were no angels and no freedom. One night my mother took me to the forest so I could walk. I started doing cartwheels just to feel peace again, and then I puked. My mother didn't know what to do. She called the inkblot psychiatrist and she advised that my mother take me to the mental facility in Münsingen, Bern. Lights out.

2

Mental Hospital in Münsingen, Bern (The Camp for Gifted Adults)

The Year 1996 Autumn

> "There is a fine line between being insane
> and being misunderstood;
> I am on the line so that makes me just fine"
>
> —*Livia Moser*

My mother, Carmen and I arrived at 02:00 in the morning and the counsellor introduced herself with her last name only. Instinctively I said, "Hi Nelly how are you?" All of them looked at me stunned, until she finally asked me "How do you know my name?" I replied "Bernard told me about you, you were his ex-girlfriend and he showed me pictures of you." My mother and sister were relieved that I wasn't psychic with special powers, but just insane.

After that I don't remember much. I don't know what they gave me but for the first 3 weeks I was so drugged up. I woke up one day tied to the bed. It reminded me of the song *"One"* by Metallica, especially the part *"can't remember anything, can't tell if this is true or dream, deep down inside I feel to scream."*

My mother and Nelly (Bernard's ex-girlfriend) were there. I asked Nelly if she had slept with Bernard. Though Nelly was embarrassed she answered honestly and said that she had.

I looked around me and I had a really nice room with my own bathroom. But however you want to put it; it was still solitary confinement (5-star solitary confinement). I had to eat all my meals in my room. I could open the windows, but only half way. Now I was furious. What had I done to be treated like a criminal? I kicked the locked door. It didn't work, so I became artistic. Luckily I had some red lipstick in my purse upon entry. I took it and painted the whole door with it. Mostly I drew hearts.

When my favourite nurse Nelly came to give me my meal, she was impressed with my artwork. It was rubbed off the next day. But I continued to draw on the door and they continued to rub it off.

The head doctor came to see me in my room and he informed me that I was schizophrenic. I didn't really understand, because I didn't have two personalities.

Since I was completely drugged up, I couldn't ask the most logical question, which was, how did he come up with this diagnosis? So I accepted it, because what did I know and doctors know everything.

He prescribed Leponex to me, a drug that is illegal in Finland and attacks the white blood cells. Since it does this, I had to get my blood tested every week. Years later I read that Leponex shouldn't be prescribed to people who have kidney problems. I don't remember having a complete health check.

Maybe I already had a faulty kidney back then, but I didn't know and certainly the doctors didn't check the physical aspect of my body. They just gave me a label and the pills to go with it. But there is a huge difference between this and choosing the right shoes to go with the appropriate dress. So I took it for the following 4 years, because the doctors know best.

Finally he seemed to have checked me off on his 'to do' list of 'new psychos to care for and sedate.' Only then was I finally allowed to leave my room. The other patients were all on the balcony smoking cigarettes and they greeted me like an old friend. I introduced myself and they did the same. Soon enough we told each other why we were in here, our past, and we probably shared more information with each other in five minutes than some people do in months.

They were a nice bunch of people. We also started to share everything, exchange clothes, jewellery or shoes. We were a family and we had to help each other out. There was no competition between us. There were also no fights.

That was the great thing of being in a mental hospital that you hardly ever hear about. All the movies I have seen, they only portray the worst. In mental hospitals people are real and their compassion is greater than outside of the mental hospitals. No one wears a mask. If they feel like crying they cry. It was the same thing with all other emotions. You are free to express exactly how you feel.

When I was sad there was always someone to cheer me up. We were all in the same boat and we were a real team who stuck together. No one would talk behind your back. There were no mind games because everyone was out of their minds. In the outside world people wore masks, but in an artificial environment like a mental hospital no one did or could. No one could walk around acting or thinking they're hot shit; they were in a mental hospital for God's sake.

I was in the corridor when Isabella showed up. She was full of life and very similar to me. She was even born in the same year and same month as me. She immediately became my best friend at camp. We were always together, talking and singing, but most of all laughing at dirty jokes. We also rated every single male in the mental hospital. Our favourite place to hang out was in the smoker's lounge right next to the radio. All we did was sing along to the songs that were being played on the radio. She was Mariah Carey and I was Whitney Houston. Her favourite song of Mariah Carey was *"Hero"* and years later I understood *"because the hero lies in you."*

The highlight of our week was when Isabella and I went swimming in the indoor pool with one gorgeous male nurse. To top it off he was a kind man. Isabella and I loved it when he took us swimming. We couldn't care less about swimming; we were mainly there to stare at his hot body. He probably noticed, because we didn't even bother hiding it.

Don't think I didn't want to escape though. It was a locked ward. One day I had my chance as the door was opened wide to let someone in. I ran as fast as I could, but I only reached the pond in the mini golf course. I jumped in it. A male nurse came to fish me out. I called him Bruce because he looked like Bruce Willis. Well he was the Swiss version. Bruce pulled me out and took me back. All the nurses were really cool, both male and female.

Bernard came to see me in the clinic; he also informed me that he had a new girlfriend. I was cool about it. I kind of realized that he wasn't my soul mate and that in my mania I had made everything up and interpreted the messages to suit me. But it was real to me at the time and who's to say it wasn't? Also I am more of a city girl than a farmer girl. So that was the end of it. I never saw him again after that, but God remained.

One day I returned to my room and there was a very old lady sitting on my toilet. I had seen her walking around the mental hospital. She had arrived a week ago. Since she had one foot in the grave she didn't have much to talk about. The following day she came into my room and said that my room was a complete mess and that I should clean it up. My mother and sister were both in the room when she came to tell me that I was a messy girl and it was hysterical.

The day after, I found her in my bed. I wasn't going to kick her out, but I wanted to take a nap, so I told a counsellor to take her out. I told him that I couldn't remove her, because I would probably break her bones and he was glad as well that I didn't remove her myself. She was cool. The mystery for me remains why was she in a mental hospital and not in an old age home? I guess she wanted to have some fun before she died. You go great granny.

There was also this farmer woman and she kept doing funny signs in the air. She kept calling me Diana, until another guy got so fed up that he told her off and said that my name was Livia and not Diana the Princess. Nevertheless she continued calling me Diana. But she was unique and the kind of lovable woman who always has hot chocolate ready for you with cookies.

The arrival of Frank brought new excitement to our camp. Isabella and I thought he was a new nurse, but he was also a patient. He was a junkie. He came and sat with us to eat and we all got on like a house on fire. He soon became my vacation boyfriend and Isabella's at the same time. What a player, but who cared, we were all crazy. There was no point to enforce rules of etiquette now. We never kissed, because all types of sexual contact were forbidden, so was drinking alcohol. I didn't care about that, because I had no sex drive with so much medication. We, however, did do creature comfort. That is basically hugging. Frank made that up 'creature comfort.' We did it in hiding, because you can't touch one another in a mental facility.

One day I had a complete breakdown and I cried for at least 2 hours. I felt like I was at the bottom of a black hole and I would be there forever. Nelly had seen me crying and she started crying to. She realized then that with me she couldn't keep the boundary between patient and counsellor. There was something in me that brought about a sense of unfairness in her that she didn't know how to deal with.

By that time we had built a relationship and I shared my ideas with her, all my hopes and plans. She saw that I was trying to always be brave and to handle everything well at such a young age. So she felt immensely sad to see me fall into such a grave hole. It was awful for me, but even more awful for her. She was trained to keep her distance, but she wasn't trained for what she was experiencing with me.

When she left the room I remembered my

favourite song, *"The Greatest Love of All."* I started to sing it and what helped me the most was the phrase *"And if by chance that special place that you have been dreaming of leads you to a lonely place find your strength in love"* I have known this song since I was 10 years old, so thank you Whitney Houston.

One weekend I was allowed to leave the camp, but on Sunday I was already bored and wanted to go back to the crazies who I partied with. Actually I had missed them. My mother took me back six hours before I was expected and a new camp member was there wearing his T-shirt from Thailand, dancing in the smoker's lounge with a non alcoholic beer. He looked like a tourist. Another guy I knew who was partying with the tourist was happy to see me and said, "Welcome back to the asylum, Livia!" I was happy to be back, because I felt like there was no place left for me outside these grounds.

I started to get used to the place, but I still wanted to leave. I knew I was not going to live there forever and had to continue on my path. I had to get to Hotel School. What I didn't realize was that you had to act normal to get out of Mental Hospitals. That is quite a paradox. You were in there because you were crazy, but to get out you had to be saner than you ever were in your whole life. I wish someone had told me sooner.

At the end of October I was moved to an open ward. I didn't like it there because the people were less interesting and the counsellors weren't as good looking as in the locked ward. There was, however, one cool guy with red long hair. He was at a point of no return. He couldn't even tell you the alphabet, but he could kick your ass on the play station. He was kind and did his own thing. I respected him for that.

My roommate was quite a character as well. When she was angry she got up early to kick the shit out of the garbage containers. Being so highly medicated it hardly disturbed me. But it made her feel better.

There was one guy who was plain weird. It was his birthday so he was allowed to travel to Bern to buy himself a present; instead he bought me a whistle that coaches use. I was touched, but I didn't know why he bought me a whistle and nothing for himself. Later I understood why he didn't buy himself a present; he knew that he was going to commit suicide. So I ask myself was he weird or smart?

What I hated the most was our Wednesday afternoon walks around the village. It was like a parade of the crazy people with escorts. I hated walking, so that didn't help either. The counsellors tried to make it more fun, by stopping for a coffee break and a pastry. The whole thing was pathetic, pitiful and pointless.

One Wednesday in December as we were walking through the village, we saw some kids playing and they were excited because Santa Clause was coming to town. In Switzerland he comes on the 6th of December. As usual I walked with the red headed guy. He shouted out to them that Santa doesn't exist. The children just stared back at him and I burst out laughing. I laughed so hard and so loud that the nurses got pissed off. They told me to please quiet down.

Then I had to attend pottery class twice a week. All I made were ashtrays. The teacher asked me, "Don't you want to try something else like a vase?" I wasn't interested in making anything else. I was good at making ashtrays. I also didn't like pottery class. I was too highly medicated to be motivated or interested.

Finally after four months I was allowed to leave the mental facility in Münsingen. The ironic thing was that when I was 13, my friends in the International School of Bern would jokingly say, you belong in Münsingen. I guess they were right, because 5 years later I ended up there.

During those 4 months many people visited me. My friends came from far and wide. They didn't drop me like a hot rock, because I was crazy. I was luckier than some of the people I had met who were abandoned by their family and friends.

My mother came to visit me every single day I was there at exactly 2 p.m. She never failed to come and only one day was she late. She was late because she had forgotten to blow out the candles in the apartment, so she drove back to blow them out. What an amazing woman. My father couldn't come everyday because he was working in Pakistan, but when he was in Switzerland he would join my mother on her daily visits. Those four months showed me how many people loved me and that makes all the difference.

I was diagnosed as a schizophrenic and I had the medication for schizophrenia. But that didn't mean that was the end of my treatment. I was promoted to a day clinic in Bern and I could live at home. I lived with my mother and younger sister who was going to high school at the International School of Bern.

3

Day Clinic (Day School for Imbeciles)

The Year 1994 Winter/Spring

"Great spirits
have always found violent opposition
from mediocre minds."
—*Albert Einstein*

I hated every minute of the day clinic. The counsellors sucked, the doctors sucked and the other patients sucked. It sucked so much that I don't remember anyone. It was so pathetic that I am not even going to waste my time and effort writing too much about it.

I don't know how I survived those six months. It was from 9:00 to 16:30, Monday to Friday. Every morning I gave the place the finger and when I left I gave the place the finger. On weekends I would sleep. On rare occasions I went to see a movie with a friend.

One activity was to play volleyball. I love volleyball. But no one knew how to play correctly so it was more like ping-pong. Then there was also moving to music (dance therapy), which was a joke. The lady would give us these ridiculous objects like a scarf, stick or a ball. Then she would play this weird music and we had to move with it. I guess it was supposed to be some form of complementary therapy, but it was ridiculous. She should have put some good music on and made us really shake our ass to get our frustrations out instead of making us even more frustrated with her boring tunes.

We also had arts and crafts. That was when we all had a huge piece of paper and we were told to draw pictures of our hopes. I drew as quickly as possible. My only hope was to get out of there.

Every week a group of us had to cook lunch. It was another so called therapy. I call it 'counsellors are too lazy to cook so use the patients.' That meant walking to the supermarket, buying the food and then cooking it. We always had a counsellor's help. If you consider help being that the counsellor pretended to be a head chef and gives orders only.

Don't bother asking me what I liked the most because there was absolutely nothing that I liked. Actually there was one thing I liked, and that was the very last day. When I said good-bye, I walked out and never looked back.

My family were all called in one day to meet the head doctor. He had a chart and he explained that only 2% of schizophrenics have a chance of a normal life. Way to go asshole! You really know how to give my family hope. I had no respect for him whatsoever because he had one of those huge home made buttons of his cat on his shirt. What self respecting doctor would put a picture of his cat on his shirt??????? How was he able to respect my family or me?

One day I had to go and do an I.Q test. My results were average, so he informed me that I shouldn't go to hotel management school because I wasn't smart enough to attend. When he told me this I just thought I am going whether you like it or not you idiot. First of all he tested me in Swiss German, when my language is unofficially English and more importantly he needed to get laid and pronto.

My personal counsellor with her extremely tight red leather pants that gave her a camel foot crotch told me the same and she suggested that I should stay in the shit hole longer. She came up with this diagnosis from the fact that I couldn't clean the table properly after lunch had been served. So that was a clear indicator that I was still sick. Where did this woman get her qualifications from, the internet? She told the same to my mother, but my mother informed her that I couldn't do this task when I was well either!

I decided then and there that I wasn't going to stay in this "nightmare of a fun house" any longer. So that's when I put my talents as an actress into first gear. I put my personality away and became a well-behaved, boring plane Jane. It worked. I was released and I was allowed to start Hotel School, a year late but I was starting.

Despite what the professionals said I was going to Hotel School and as hard as they had tried they didn't achieve in dissuading me to go. It only made my firm resolve stronger. Their opinions were immediately flushed down my mental toilet as soon as they stated them. It was this mechanism that made me able to believe that I could be normal, intelligent and most of all a useful member in society. So screw em all!!!!! Sorry, but I was furious.

Walking out of there on my last day after 6 long excruciating months was fantastic and looking back I think it was the only day I was actually happy in those months. They were the worst months in my life so far and I would have traded living in Pakistan again for them. I would have even preferred to have been in the locked ward for 6 months. They should have given me a T-shirt for staying there with 'I survived the day clinic' written on it.

Hotel Management School

The Year 1995 Autumn

"Live as if your were to die tomorrow.
Learn as if you were to live forever."
—*Gandhi*

This was it! I was starting hotel school. My mother was driving me up to my school, which used to be a hotel nestled in the beautiful countryside of eastern Switzerland. I had seen the school before I got ill and I just knew I would like it there.

My confidence was, however, shaky and I went over and over again what to tell people if they asked me what I had done for the past year. I couldn't say "Hi I am Livia and I have just been released from 10 months of mental care." Also I was 19 and I was ashamed. I was only confronted once with that question when we all had to introduce ourselves in class. I told everyone that I had travelled and taken a German course. The German course part was true.

I was also nervous for the first test. Could I pass, did I still have my intelligence or was I really stupid like the I.Q guy had said. When I scored 5.5 out of 6 that solved everything. All my doubts were gone and I became confident again. I was myself again, crazy and fun. I did really well in school.

The only problem was that the pills would make me tired and when I woke up I went to class looking like a disaster. I used to fall asleep in the morning classes. People used to make fun of me, but I was always able to laugh at myself. They weren't mean to me and I was well liked by my teachers and the student body.

The semester went by smoothly and I noticed there were more psychos in that school than me. Well they could blame their craziness on being drunk. I, however, was born drunk. Just like Obelix who fell into the cauldron of strength, I had fallen into the cauldron of happiness. It was strange how everyone else was drinking to get happy and I was taking pills to not be too happy. So I was literally taking chill pills.

It was time to pack up and leave for winter vacation. During my vacation I woke up one morning and went to the bathroom. I saw that my urine was the colour of red wine. Luckily my father saw it otherwise I would have ignored it. We went to the doctor. There was something wrong with my kidneys. The Doctor hoped it wasn't that bad. It was too early to tell what the problem was. She gave me some pills and I continued with my life.

The time for the second semester had come and I was happy to go back to school. Seeing all my friends again was great. I noticed that people loved to complain about everything they could. The food wasn't good; the rooms weren't renovated; blah, blah and so forth. Also a lot of the students would continuously complain how bored they were, but they wouldn't find anything to entertain themselves. I kept myself busy doing sports. Monday night was indoor soccer and Thursday night was volleyball. The student bar was open on Wednesdays, Fridays, and Sundays. I would be the first to arrive and the last to leave.

I was lucky that my Grandma lived near me in the village where I come from officially. I had to see the village doctor quite frequently about my kidney function. My Nana would pay for the taxi ride back to school. In April I had to go to the hospital for four days to do a kidney biopsy and it really hurt. My friends came to visit, so did my mother.

I had a consultation with the Head of the Nephrology Department. He asked me if I wanted to take cortisone or not? What kind of question is that to ask of a 19-year-old girl? I said if it will help my kidney I'll take it. It didn't help my kidney but it turned my face into J.Lo's ass. My cheeks were so puffed up. Luckily I am not a vain person otherwise I would never have left my room.

The 2nd semester also ran smoothly and I had a good time. But mostly everyone was trying to find a place for their in-training. I found a job in a 39-bedroom hotel. When I was at the interview I had no idea what I was getting into. If I knew what it would be like I would have never signed the contract.

I had one month of summer vacation before I started my in-training.

5

The Practicum of Hell in Lucerne

01.7.1996–30.7.1997

"Arguing with a fool proves there are two."
—*Doris M. Smith*

My mother drove me to the hotel. I had a small room in the hotel with a television and my own bathroom. That was good, but I was also paying for it. This was the toughest year of my life. It was a real challenge and I had a boss from hell. I wonder who was running hell while I was there.

He would shout at me every single day. The way I dealt with it was that I would go to my room, take my uniform off and put my clothes on. I would also put some make up on and go out to eat in a restaurant. After that everything was forgotten. If I didn't respect someone I couldn't get hurt by them. Not once did I cry. I was also lucky that the exploited Portuguese staff were so kind to me.

Basically what I had to do was wake up at 6:00 in the morning, heat up the frozen croissants, prepare the breakfast buffet, take telephone calls and check people out at the reception. I was a one-woman show at that hotel (just my pager and me). Guests used to ask me when they were checking out, are you the only person who works here? Then I would have to wait until the asshole would show up. It was mostly between 13:00 to 15:00; whenever he felt like showing up. After 18:00 I would have to wait in my room for him to call me until the tour group had arrived. I would then serve a three-course dinner to the tour group.

The hardest time was during the three days of carnival when I was working sixteen hours a day, three days in a row. My feet were killing me. I also did the dishes for the Portuguese staff. I was wondering if that diploma was worth all this. But I was never going to quit. I was going to pull through come hell or high water.

The fondest memory I have was of Christmas Eve; I had to work, so I couldn't be with my family. The Portuguese staff invited me to their home. They were poor, but they had the heart to know I was alone. For that gesture I will always be grateful, even if the food was bad. I mean who eats alphabet soup at

Christmas? But I didn't care. They could have served me a cracker and I would have been happy.

I also made friends with a man and a woman at the souvenir store on the same street. They were my two angels, where I could vent my frustrations. The lady was from Thailand and sometimes she would bring me food. It made me realize that no matter what kind of hell I was going through there were always others who cared. The people I cared about, I remember well. I can't even remember half of the cruel words my boss told me.

One guy I really liked was Hong. He was Thai and the owner's boyfriend. One day he came to me and said "I go Thailand with Loland for thlee weeks bye bye." His accent was hilarious and the fact that I lived in Bangkok, Thailand, made us immediate friends. (I understand now why they call Bangkok the city of angels). He showed me all his jewellery and told me how much it cost. "Look Livia, Loland (the boss) buy this faw me, it cot 10 thouland flanc at buchelel (Bucherer is an expensive jewellery shop in Switzerland)."

One evening at work The Boss came in and said to Hong "say bye to Mummy", Hong said "bye Mummy". It was definitely clear to see who was using who in this relationship. It was Hong and Hong was kind to me. He knew that I knew he was using the boss and he didn't mind. All I wanted to do was applaud him for using the boss, because he was such an asshole.

Near the end of my in-training, a lady from the chocolate store on the same street as the hotel asked me how I had managed a year with the owner. She told me that other employees lasted only a week or two. I guess I managed because I don't get hurt easily. I think only people you love can hurt you.

When I spoke to my sister Sarah, in Canada, I told her that finishing this in-training would be like really having to take a big shit and then the relief when you have done it. Symbolically on the last day I took a big shit after I was done working. It was the happiest day of my life. I had done it. I had survived. I was really proud of myself. The kind of pride when it doesn't matter who else is proud of you. To celebrate I took my younger sister out to eat a pizza. My mother gave me flowers because she heard much of my ranting and raving throughout the whole year.

During the year I still had to visit a doctor for my kidney and the pills for my psyche. He was a good doctor and reduced some of my pills, so I was more energetic. Every month I had to bring him a collection of 24-hour urine. I had the urine in a huge flask and I walked through Lucerne with it.

I would have loved to be mugged carrying the urine and just seeing the image of the thief's face when he saw that all he stole was urine. That thought cracked me up every single time I went to deliver the urine to get it checked at the lab. This incident never happened, but it made me laugh.

To reward myself I bought a ticket to the United States to visit my best friend whom I hadn't seen in 10 years. I also went to visit my sister in Canada. I had a blast and was ready to go back to the Hotel School.

6

Great Times in Hotel Management School

The Years 1997–1998

"Be happy while you're living, for you're a long time dead."
—*Scottish Proverb*

This was my senior year in Hotel School and it was the best year. I had more energy because my psycho pills had been reduced. There was also a better group of people. Also a Canadian guy joined. He was married, but we were really good friends and we were always together. He was really funny and smart. So I always had a beer buddy at the bar.

If we had an exam the next day, we would study and meet at a certain hour. It was our routine. Our classmates would ask, "Don't you know there is a test tomorrow?" It was always the same story. If I wrote about Hotel School that would be another book, so I will keep it short.

Overall it was a good year. I had good grades. Partied a lot and arranged activities. I still did sports. Before I knew it, graduation arrived and I was the class speaker because no one else wanted to do it. I loved making speeches. The most disappointing thing about graduation was that the people who couldn't wait to get out of there cried the most. I kept thinking why are they crying, these people couldn't wait to leave? I always liked it there and I didn't cry at all. I am not a 'don't know what you've got till it's gone' kind of girl.

I was in a dilemma after graduation. I knew I had to live in Switzerland because of my health, but I had such an international upbringing that the Swiss didn't get me. I had a completely different sense of humour than the Swiss. It was then that I realized that the hardest thing about being an expatriate daughter is when you feel there is more 'culture shock' in your own country from your own nationals than in other places you've lived.

This is due to the fact that you are mentally prepared for culture shock and people tell you about it, but no one talks about reverse culture shock. The amounts of my friends who have suffered from reverse culture shock are numerous. There is even a label for kids like us 'global privileged orphans' (no that is a joke or a term I invented). The real term is 'third culture kids'. Great another label for me! What is it with people and labels?

So I chose the most international city in Switzerland and that was Geneva. The hurdle was that I didn't speak French at that time, but I was going to learn. The positive side was that Geneva was where all the 'third culture kids' lived and now some of them are my friends.

7

Another Foreigner (Me) Resides in Geneva

Summer/Autumn 1998

"Medicine being a compendium of the successive and contradictory mistakes of medical practitioners, when we summon the wisest of them to our aid, the chances are that we may be relying on a scientific truth the error of which will be recognized in a few years' time."

—*Marcel Proust*

My older sister had finished doing her MBA in Canada, so she thought she would come to Geneva as well. She found a job and a fiancé on the spot. I found a great apartment for my sister, my then best friend and myself. I liked Geneva. It was more laid back than the rest of Switzerland and there were so many nationalities present. I felt right at home here since I was always a foreigner in my own country, so why stop now? I went to the University of Geneva to do a nine-week intensive course in French. I learnt enough, but it still took me 5 months to find a job in a hotel as a receptionist.

Luckily during that time, Sava the penis cartoonist was living with us. So I had company. We had a great time together, because we had the same sense of humour. My younger sister was studying nearby in another hotel management school. She would come and visit us with her gay friend. She came on the weekends because she liked Sava.

Her gay friend also had to vent his gayness, because he had to be in the closet back at hotel school. He was 'in your face' gay, but he was funny and we all liked him. There was also another frequent visitor to our pad. He was from California and he would always bring olives and wine. He knew so many dirty jokes. I also knew dirty jokes so once in awhile the jokes would roll and everyone would laugh. There was much laughter in that apartment.

In late October, I went to see how my kidneys were doing. I went to the hospital in Geneva. The professor of the nephrology department didn't understand why I was on Cortisone. So he called the other doctor who prescribed it to me. The next day that doctor called and told me I could stop taking the pills. He had made a mistake and wanted to cover it up.

The professor in Geneva also sent me to a

psychiatrist. I told her that I was on Leponex, a drug for schizophrenics. I wanted to reduce this and eventually eliminate the dose. I had been on this drug for four years. She also realized that I wasn't a schizophrenic, but had more hypo maniac tendencies. Great! Another wrong diagnosis!!!! Also I was disappointed that I couldn't send myself a Valentine's card the following year stating roses are red, violets are blue, I am schizophrenic and so am I. She started to reduce the medication so that I could finally be without medication.

I finally got a job as a receptionist in a 5 star hotel in November. I liked working there. My life was going really well. I had my first real job and when I called my father he cried. I met many interesting people and lunatics. I worked a lot of late shifts. So when I got home at midnight everyone else was in bed.

A fond memory was New Year's Eve 1998. My two sisters and three of our friends all went to a night club and drank and danced until 05.00 in the morning. One of my fantasies came true that night.

I saw a guy across the dance floor, locked eyes, danced and then we kissed. There was only one problem. We didn't speak any common language. I felt like God was laughing at me. The next day his friend, the translator, called me to arrange a meeting. I told him kindly that there was really no point if we couldn't even communicate verbally.

January came and at the end I was on no

medication, I also had a crush on this new guy working in the hotel, he was a cook. Another guy started harassing me at the reception even though he worked in a different department. I told him not to do it again.

One evening I went for a break and fainted, he picked me up and kissed me. With my last remaining strength I pushed him away. I looked at myself in the mirror and it was turning tomato red. I felt like my life was in danger so I ran to my locker and when I opened it there were handcuffs in it. What were the handcuffs doing in there? I had no idea where they came from? I was sure I didn't put them in there, because I didn't even own a pair of handcuffs.

I called an old love of mine and he told me to relax and breathe. Just to hear his voice reassured me. The last time I had seen him was in London singing *"Nothing Else Matters"* in the bathtub together and having a great night together in the summer. Then he told me something strange. "The traffic in Geneva is worse than in London." Did he mean that he was in Geneva to come to my rescue? I was confused.

I knew what I had to do; I had to get the hell out of there and fast. I quit during my trial period, by leaving a note to the General Manager. I asked the concierge to call me the best cab to drive me home. Another strange thing happened, the taxi driver didn't charge me for the cab fare. That's probably because I was singing out the window.

The next day I told my sister that I was sick and that she should take me to the mental facility. I knew I was euphoric again. My mother was called. Both my parents were living in Pakistan. She flew in immediately to take care of me. The biggest fear for other people is that you will die, because of reckless behaviour. I agree with that because you do feel immortal. So I was again under supervision.

I was happy though living in my fantasy world. One time my arm hurt so I called the ambulance. They asked me what happened; I replied, "I fell...... in love." The problem is they didn't react like I was crazy. Was I blind? If someone told me that, I would give an expression of confusion. But these ambulance people acted like this happened everyday. That is why I couldn't really grasp that I was insane. People didn't react to me like I was crazy and they didn't treat me like I was crazy. Maybe they were just really polite and didn't want to say anything unethical.

8

From Patient to Receptionist

The Year 1999

"We may have all come on different ships,
but we're in the same boat now."
—*Martin Luther King, Jr.*

In February my shrink asked me if I wanted to go to a private clinic in Nyon. I agreed, because I didn't want to hang around my mother anymore and wanted some freedom.

When I arrived at the private clinic, freedom was the last thing I had. I was once again put in a locked ward called after the Geneva Lake which in French is called Lac Leman. I called it Le Man, in other words the man. I immediately called my shrink who asked me if I wanted to go there and furiously asked her why I was in the locked ward when I came here voluntarily. She didn't have an answer for me.

Leman was as suicide proof as possible. I couldn't even have my own lighter. Every time I wanted to light my cigarette I had to ask a nurse. So no one could attempt to kill himself or herself. One guy decided to become creative and almost did. He broke the toothbrush glass and tried to cut himself with the shards.

I saw this event and called the nurses. They came like a bunch of seagulls and flocked on him like he was a breadcrumb. It was quite incredible. I had to say, however, that the grounds were really impressive and so were the facilities. It was also expensive. The food was excellent and I was always happy to see steak and French-fries on the menu with of course my favourite ketchup brand.

This time I was lucky, because upon entry there was a nice man who gave me a good piece of advice. He said, "Behave yourself and you will be out of here in no time." I listened to his advice. I never acted up even though I was still in my mania. After all I had a job to do. Fight the devil and save the world again.

At least I thought I was fighting the Devil. One day I got so angry that I called the guy that I thought loved me and said, "I am here fighting the devil and you are fucking your girlfriend." What a complete fool I made of myself. I knew he had a girlfriend. But try to tell that to a crazy person. He basically told me to get lost and to never call him again. So I lost all contact with him, just because I was in a mania again.

The people I met there were amazing. It seemed that the more they suffered in their lives, the kinder they were. They also had the biggest hearts. I was truly amazed.

There was a lady who was raped (when she was younger by a relative.) A 13-year old boy raped her 9-year old son and when she found this out she threw herself into Lake Geneva in winter. Her husband found her. She was really kind and loved to paint my fingernails. She told me her story and I was very sad for her. The only thing I could do for her was to make her laugh. That was my strength making people laugh so I used it whenever I could.

Another girl who looked like an angel with her blonde curly hair and bright blue eyes was anorexic and she used to cut herself. Her father sexually abused her. I decided that I was going to be her protector. I felt like a lioness protecting her cub. Even though she had gone through so many traumas at such a young age, she still managed to laugh and smile.

At that time I also had a great connection with God, and God had a funny sense of humour. I asked God to send a tall brown-haired guy to join me at the Leman (the locked ward). The very next day the candidate came. I was really exited, but there was only one problem, he never spoke, all he did was read books. I went up to him and asked him, "What is your name?" He replied in his pipsqueak voice, "Stephane". So I asked God to bring me the same again, but this time someone who speaks.

You have to be very clear what you ask from God; otherwise he will definitely make fun of you. The next day another candidate came and God had got it right this time.

He spoke a lot and we became fast friends. His name was Robert and he played the guitar. At night he would play some kind of melody and I would make up the lyrics. We made 4 songs. The lyrics didn't make any sense, but it helped make the time pass.

Robert had tried to kill himself and that was the reason why he was in Leman. He just couldn't handle reality and the carousel of daily life. To say he was a dreamer was an understatement.

Robert finally managed to kill himself. I called him a couple of years later and his stepfather answered the phone. I asked if I could speak to Robert. His stepfather told me that Robert had killed himself. He had driven himself off a cliff. My first reaction was, well I guess I am not having a drink with Robert today or any other day. I did feel sad, but also happy for him. He was in a better place, jamming on his guitar.

Then Therese showed up. She was in an open ward but some male nurse sexually harassed her. She suffered from anxiety attacks. One time we were eating and she had a panic attack. I reached over, hugged her tight and told her that the white horse was here. I used the white horse, because she wrote beautiful fairytales of this white horse. She calmed down and the attack passed. She was also a very nice girl and we had a good group going at the Leman.

I returned from a weekend outside of the clinic when I noticed that a male patient had a bandage on his cheek. I immediately went up to him and asked him what had happened. He didn't want to talk about it. So I asked the anorexic angel. She told me that he tried to shoot himself over the weekend, but the bullet went through the cheek and not to the brain. It was so sad that it was funny.

One man I particularly liked; he looked like a cowboy with his rugged looks. But he was deeply depressed and every time I wanted to hug him to comfort him, there would be some nurse to say, "Madame Moser! Not too close, no touching". Did you have to try to kill yourself to feel another human's touch? What kind of fucked up rule was that? It wasn't like I was kissing him or anything.

Since I was promoted to leave the ward twice a day for half an hour, I didn't feel like transferring to an open ward. Also the people in the open ward were much older than me. In the main hall, I met other people who were from different wards and I spoke to everyone. That is just the way I am. I learnt a lot about human suffering and how much humans could actually handle.

The shrinks there were alright. They didn't give me much hope. They weren't the cheerleader types.

It would have been nice to have a shrink tell me "Go Livia, you can do it, no matter what." But they never said that. I was lucky that I had a goal which was my dream hotel. This dream was like the northern star in the dark night to always guide me. But what about the other young people who didn't have a dream or goal? The shrinks could destroy their confidence. That is the problem of society. We think doctors are gods, but they are only human and they too make mistakes. My experience has shown me that doctors can screw up big time.

I was supposed to check out after 4 weeks, but my mother told the shrink that I wasn't ready. I was so furious with her that I told her I never wanted to see her again. I cried after that, I felt really betrayed. How could my mother go behind my back? She must have had her reasons. So I was able to leave after 6 weeks in total. I was able to go home, but I was so exhausted and my motivation was low. All I wanted to do was sleep. And that is exactly what I did.

One thing about mental hospitals is that you make intense friendships, but when you leave so do those friendships. It is rare that you see these people again. It isn't a rule, but it's like you are getting off a boat that went through a storm and you don't want to go back on it with the survivors.

I was happy and sad to leave. I would miss these people who had shared their stories with me and me with them. We had laughed and cried together. But this wasn't the reality that I wanted. I wanted to go back to working in hotels. Oh by the way, I killed the devil on the 22nd of March 1999.

I bet you want to know how I killed him. Well I am going to tell you. I killed him with my super human powers of white magic and not accepting to go to his side. His endless whisperings of, "If God loves you so much why would he lock you up and if you joined me I would give you the hotel you dreamed of." The devil started to piss me off, he just couldn't handle rejection. Even after I kindly said no and told him that he was a liar and I am sticking with God and the truth. I also told him to go back to hell and leave my friends and me alone.

The world was once again at peace, or so I thought. The philosophy of "I think therefore I am" doesn't apply to me. In a mania it is "I think therefore I am not." I seriously believed there was world peace, but wars were still going on in the world. I was heartbroken.

When I arrived home to the same apartment which used to have so much laughter it was now barren. My sister and my friend had moved out. It was only my mother and I now living there. So I slept for about two months. I can't remember what happened. I preferred to sleep. It's always the same with me. I get really happy, go to the mental hospital, get drugged up, and get depressed. But I knew I couldn't live this way and that I had to find a job and live again.

In August I found a job as a receptionist in a 3-star hotel. I didn't like the interior decoration, but I was offered the job on the spot and I took it. The first months were a disaster. I hated working there. I was also unhappy and not comfortable in my skin. That is the biggest hell on earth; being unhappy in your skin. I didn't do a good job; in fact I did a half-assed job. I got a warning letter from the General Manager who was female. It was basically shape up or ship out, of course sugar-coated. That was a real kick in the ass for me. I thought about looking for another job and I only sent one application, but I didn't get the other job, so I decided to work harder. I was also too fat. I had to lose weight. I did so by not putting sugar in my coffee and only eating one main meal a day.

9

Climbing the Ladder Just to See it Crumble Beneath You

The Year 2000

"Expecting life to treat you well
because you are a good person
is like expecting an angry bull not to charge
because you are a vegetarian."

—*Shari R. Barr*

I was starting to feel really good again. I had lost weight and I improved in my job. But what made a big difference in my work life was the arrival of a new in-trainee. He was a Mexican guy and great to work with. We had a lot of fun. By that time I had become the General Manger's emotional toilet. If she was angry or stressed it was my fault. She would shout at me and she was hysterical. She was also stupid and easily threatened. So if there was anyone that was smarter than her around she would drive them into insanity, so that they would quit. I had experienced worse so she was a piece of cake to deal with.

I liked working there as the staff was really nice. We were all in the same boat, us against the witch. When the witch was in a bad mood she would find someone to shit on. I was her usual target, because I could handle her the most. I had also been there the longest. All the others had quit. The current staff hated her too. It was like being in a television series everyday. Since I am a bit of a drama queen I loved the action. The more drama the better it was. I would always ask to work weekends, because the witch wasn't there. Strangely enough the owners and the witch gave us complete freedom. She would never show up on the weekend, neither did the owners. It was our hotel and we were free to do what we wanted.

The Mexican guy and I always arranged that we worked weekends. He wanted to work in the mornings and I wanted to work in the evenings. Then we decided to shorten our hours. We each worked 7 hours instead of the full 9 that was expected of us. We also had contingency plans, in case she called. Luckily we never had to use them. It was great.

My social life was also good. I would go out. My love life wasn't happening. I don't fall in love easily, but when I do, I fall hard. I did, however, have adventures. The drugs that keep me sane do affect my sex drive so that may be it. I wasn't even interested in finding a boyfriend. But the older I got the more I could speak about my mental illness. I was no longer ashamed of it. I accepted it and that was the most important part.

Yes things were looking up for me. I was myself again and happy until I went to get a check up. My kidney wasn't doing well at all. It was at the point where only a transplant would help. Aaah shit, shit, shit!!! At that moment I wanted to die, I couldn't fight again.

My mother and I went to see a nephrologist (kidney doctor). My mother was prepared to donate her kidney to me. She had to do tests to see if we were compatible and we were. After that we went to the hospital in Geneva, which luckily is a transplant centre. We spoke to the head of the nephrology department and he told me what tests I would have to go through. The same day they did blood tests and the very next day I was called in. It was August 4th, 2000 and I had to start dialysis immediately. I could no longer work.

I had no history of this kidney illness in my family and how was it possible that in a matter of five years, my kidneys could degenerate so quickly. Out of those five years, four of them I was on the wrong medication (Leponex), because of a wrong diagnosis, so of course I was suspicious. I asked the kidney specialists if that could be a reason, but of course they said there was no correlation.

My mother and I went to a lawyer to see what we could do against the doctors, but he said that it was too hard to fight the doctors legally and we would just spend too much money. So I felt helpless, because there was nothing I could do.

I had to take all kinds of tests for the transplant. My heart, lungs, eyes, veins, vagina and bones had to be checked. They also did an AIDS test and that is the only time when I am glad that I am not positive. I also had to take vaccinations. This had become my full time job, but it was more stressful. I was under stress. I had dialysis three times a week and the tests in between. On September the 8th, 2000 I broke down. It was too much. I started crying and crying. It was also at the most inappropriate place. I broke down in the maternity ward where a friend had just given birth to a beautiful girl.

So here I was crying, while everyone was celebrating. I really tried to contain myself, but I just couldn't. The stress had caught up. The endless pinching and poking from the needles and the running around and waiting in rooms for tests had worn me down to complete exhaustion. I couldn't handle it anymore. I guess that is why I was called a patient, because I had to be patient.

The transplant was fixed for the 13th of October

2000. Since I had my catheter in my thigh it created a thrombosis and the transplant was cancelled. I was hospitalised for 2 weeks. I was put on a drip to thin my blood. But I had fun at the hospital, there were four other women there and we would always hang out at the smoker's corner and we laughed so loud that the nurses had to shut us up.

There was also a very handsome male nurse, who was extremely kind. He asked for my number, but never called. I didn't blame him. I was a patient, but then again why bother asking for my number and anyway when a guy says he will call; I always take it with a grain of salt. I didn't want a pity call.

The thrombosis was my fault because I walked around town with the catheter for dialysis in my leg, but I was twenty-four years old and I wasn't going to lie around all day. Also my morale was good. This thrombosis was so huge that it inflated my left leg. So I had two different legs. One belonged to Arnold Schwarzenegger and one was mine. I only saw this when I took a bath, because throughout the day my leg was wrapped in bandages.

With all this stress I went crazy. I had to save the world again. I was sent to the state mental facility, which I didn't like. All we could do was smoke. There were no extracurricular activities, unless you call smoking an extracurricular activity.

Now I was really cornered, I had three illnesses at once, all potentially fatal. Without the dialysis machine I would be dead in twelve days. The thrombosis could move to my lungs or heart and kill me and manias make you feel immortal. All I could think was who the hell is after me? Who wants to see me dead? I was only twenty-four, what would the rest of my life be like? What was next, cancer? Was I going to have a career in being ill? I started to believe that I was under a curse. This was not normal. As Bon Jovi would say I was *"Living on a Prayer"* and just listening to the song helped me get over the difficulties facing me. I had myself and that's a lot for love I'll give it a shot. There was nothing else to do but fight for survival.

Since I was under a mania I couldn't even be on the kidney waiting list. In my mania I decided that I didn't want my mother's kidney and that I wanted to wait. I wrote a four-page letter to my mother explaining why I didn't want her kidney. She didn't take it well. I understood her reaction. She must have thought that I was rejecting her. I also wrote a letter to my father explaining my reasons.

I didn't want my mother's kidney for many reasons. What if something happened to her during the operation? What if I would reject the kidney? And I didn't want to be indebted to her for the rest of my life. I thought about it long and hard and finally I knew that this was the best choice.

Now the next problem was that I wasn't allowed to be on the waiting list for two years. That was what my shrink said. Thinking it was complete bullshit, I silently swore to myself that I wasn't waiting that long just to get on that list. So it was again the same routine, act saner than anyone on the planet really is.

10

Getting in the Waiting Line

The Year 2001

"Never take life seriously.
Nobody gets out alive anyways."
—*Anonymous*

I continued with my really sane act and since it worked I was put on the list on April Fools Day 2001. (Yeah I know ironic) I went back to work halftime at the same hotel in January. Of course I still had dialysis 3 times a week for four hours each session. I called my dialysis machine Jimmy. I went on Mondays, Wednesdays and Friday mornings. I dealt with dialysis the best way I could. I went to sleep at 4:00 in the morning and woke up at 07:30. I went to the hospital exhausted; the nurses hooked me up to the machine. I had breakfast in bed and I fell asleep.

I started rating my sessions. When I had to be

woken up by a nurse to inform me that dialysis was over, that was a ten. Sometimes I woke up fifteen minutes before the end. Every minute on that machine felt like eternity. The minutes would never go by. Those would be eights. The lousiest sessions were when I couldn't fall asleep or my blood pressure would drop making me feel queasy and hot.

After dialysis I would always take a taxi home. It wasn't far to where I lived, but I didn't feel like walking or taking the bus. In all those times of taxi riding home no taxi driver complained except this one asshole. He had the worst car. He asked me, "Aren't you ashamed to take a taxi for such a short distance?" I told him that I just had dialysis. He told me that I could only do that because the Swiss had stolen Jewish gold. I was really angry, but I didn't have the energy to fight with him.

Mostly when the taxi drivers dropped me off I would almost crawl into the apartment and hit the couch. My mother was always there to cook me a meal following the dialysis handbook of what I could eat and what I couldn't eat. I had to be careful of the volume of water that I drank. Because the water would not leave my body, I could gain two kilos in two days. Once I gained eight kilos in three days, the doctors weren't pleased. They couldn't take all the water out in one sitting of dialysis, because it would be too heavy on the heart.

I was very grateful that my mother was always

there to cook for me, because I could then go to work at 16:30. She took very good care of me. When I went to work I looked like a healthy young woman. My life was an awful joke. In the morning I was in the hospital hooked to this machine with blood passing through a filter and back again. If I didn't go to dialysis I would be dead in twelve days. Later I was a groomed receptionist without a care in the world. At least I am sure that is what a lot of people thought of me. But working was good for me, because I needed contact with the outside world.

Another problem I had during my dialysis was that I would have periods for 9 months. They weren't heavy. If I had known earlier I would have bought shares in the company that manufactures the pads of my preference.

It wasn't always easy and I was the youngest in my dialysis centre by far. I enjoyed the reaction from external doctors who came into the dialysis centre, old person, old person, even older man, young girl. The doctors almost took a step backward, like I was in the wrong room or something. Yes it was a sight to see.

The best thing about having kidneys that didn't work was that I never had to go to the bathroom while watching a movie.

In May the hospital called me to tell me that they had a kidney for me. Great I thought, not one single family member is in town. So I called my sister's boyfriend. He reassured me and said he would take care of things.

I felt a bit better, but still nervous on the way there. I showed up and they told me that the kidney went to another transplant centre so I could go home. False alarm! I didn't mind, because I wasn't mentally prepared. But if they don't have a kidney, why bother calling me, this is an organ not some department store promotion. Talk about bad organization.

At work things were still the same. The staff turnover at the reception was huge because of the witch/general manager. But the hotel staff had compassion for my illness and they cared about me. The owners always asked me if I was feeling well.

A lot of people couldn't believe that I was going to have a transplant and neither could I. This is something that happens to other people. Sometimes it felt so unreal that I was going through all this. I remember when I heard about organ donation a long time ago, I thought it was disgusting to have somebody else's organ in your body, but when you need one, all those superficial thoughts fly straight out of the window.

11

Rebirth

The Year 2002

"There are only two ways
to live your life.
One is as though
nothing is a miracle.
The other is as though
everything is a miracle."
—*Albert Einstein*

In January I got lucky. On Thursday the seventeenth of January I had sex with a guy called Luke. He had the same initials as me. After having sex we compared scars. We were both like "yeah we aren't lucky people." The paradox is that you are supposed to feel lucky if you just got laid. In the morning he walked me to the hospital, because I had dialysis. I was excited because the next day I was going to London for a restaurant opening. Everyone was going to be there. My mother and sisters were already there. I had to work on Friday afternoon so I couldn't fly with them the previous night.

I had to get up early on Saturday morning to catch my plane to London. I arrived in London and grabbed a cab to the hotel where my mother was staying. We went down for breakfast together. There was a huge buffet including either pig or cow kidney. My mother said jokingly I am going to eat what you need. We both had a good laugh. We sat down to eat breakfast when my mobile rang. It was the hospital in Geneva. They had found a kidney for me. My first reaction was give it to someone else, because I wanted to party in London. But my mother would have nothing to do with it. We were going and that was that. She was much smarter than me.

Then complete chaos broke out. Everyone was freaking out; also my battery was low on my mobile. Why is it always when you need your mobile the most that your battery is low? My mother ran down to the reception to ask for a recharger. Luckily they had one. My sister and her boyfriend were looking for flights to get back to Geneva. We found a flight, but London Heathrow was so big. We jumped into a taxi and told him to take us to our terminal. He took us to the wrong one.

So there was my mother and I running like idiots through Heathrow airport to catch our flight. I really thought I was in a movie. We finally arrived at the gate, but the airplane door had been closed. My mother freaked out at the desk clerk and said that I had to have a transplant in Geneva and had to be on that plane. We were allowed on the aircraft and we were Geneva bound.

Upon arrival in Geneva a man rushed into the aircraft and asked where Madame Moser was. I didn't have to go through passport control, because the ambulance was on the tarmac. At high speed we basically flew to the hospital with the ambulance. My mother was also enjoying the action. I wonder what the other passengers thought on that flight. I looked perfectly healthy and there was an ambulance at the tarmac for me. The other passengers must have been confused.

When we arrived at the hospital I had to undergo my final dialysis. During that time my blood and the donor's blood were being cross-matched. If we didn't match, the transplant would not go ahead. Luckily we were the perfect match and the transplant would go ahead. All the dialysis nurses who were on duty came to wish me good luck and they were so happy for me. I was probably the patient that they knew the best because I would tell them everything that was going on in my life.

I knew it was a young man's kidney, because the doctor slipped and said he instead of saying the donor. At least there was one man out there who was the perfect match.

After waiting for sixteen months, fifteen days and eleven hours it was time. The transplant took place at 07:30 on Sunday the 20th of January 2002. If I had known that having sex with Lucky Luke would have brought me a kidney I would have had sex with him much earlier.

The operation itself took two and half hours, but after that I was in intensive care. I had all sorts of tubes attached to me. I couldn't drink or eat for the following 6 hours of the operation, because the stomach is still asleep. The worst part of the whole transplant experience was the incredible thirst I had. I dreamt of taking a huge bottle of water and chugging it down or a soda with lots of ice. The thirst was unbearable, so I asked for ice cubes.

When I couldn't handle the thirst I would ask for more morphine so I could sleep. I didn't really need the morphine, because I was not in too much pain. Also there was a nurse with a lisp. I asked her when I could drink and she replied, but because of her lisp I didn't understand a word she said. This frustrated me even more. The first time I had to stand up was painful because of the scar.

Finally I was transferred into a half private room. They had pumped 11 litres of water into my body to jump-start my kidney, so when I looked in the mirror I saw Princess Fiona from *"Shrek"*, but not the pretty version. I was mortified, but I knew that I had to pee it out and that it was only water.

A lady doctor came to me and said that your kidney is not working at hundred percent. I told her that I have faith, she looked at me with a bewildered expression that this has nothing to do with the silly notion of faith little girl. This is the wonderful world of medicine. I had to laugh at that. These doctors really did think they are Gods!

I went to do another kidney biopsy and they found out that the first immunosuppressant wasn't working for me. I was happy about that because this certain immunosuppressant made you grow unwanted hair. Becoming a grizzly bear wasn't on my list. I had a kidney transplant and not a sex change. So after they changed drugs my kidney started working and it worked well. So take that you faithless lady doctor!

I was let out after three weeks and I was happy to be home. The doctors informed me that I couldn't work for three months. I had to have a lot of check ups after I was released to go home. During that time I watched a lot of movies. I also met my boyfriend a month after the transplant. He was Italian, so I went to Italy on the weekends sometimes. In April we took a one-week trip to Sardinia. We stayed at his Grandma's house and I couldn't communicate with her, because I didn't speak Italian. The way we communicated best was by laughter. She had a contagious laughter and so did I. So we would just laugh for no particular reason, but it was pleasant.

The Italians are pretty conservative but she allowed

us to sleep in the same room, well he was 38 years old. That bedroom looked more like a church than a bedroom. There were pictures of the Virgin Mary and statues of Jesus. Actually the whole heavenly family was there. Well I didn't mind there was space for all of us. It was an aphrodisiac having sex with all of them watching. I am sure if those statues could move, they would give us two thumbs up.

In May I went back to work, but this time I went full time. The summer was approaching and we barely had any staff. So again everything was my fault. I had again become the witch's emotional toilet.

After three years of this crap, I decided enough was enough and that I was going to defend myself. When I was a child my older sister defended me, so I never really learnt to defend myself. I called her up in the office and asked her politely if I could speak to her. Then I went to her office and told her that whatever I do I get yelled at. What kind of problem did she have with me? Not used to me defending myself she leaned back in her chair and said in a very phoney voice, "I have no problem with you."

After that she started asking for my resignation. I planned to leave anyway, because I knew that under her regime I would be a receptionist for the rest of my life. I made a deal with her. I told her that if she gave me a great reference letter, I would leave with no scandal. She and I knew that the owners liked me very much, so she was more than happy to oblige.

I wrote my letter of resignation for the fifteenth of December. But since I had so many vacation days and they would have to pay me that in cash, they told me to go on vacation in mid-November. I happily obliged and booked myself a ticket to visit a friend in Oslo, Norway. The staff and she gave me a nice farewell party.

I remember one time how she told me that I was basically worthless and that I should go work in a post office. She would also tell the other receptionists that I am stupid and didn't know anything. My colleagues knew better. They all saw how I worked. She was just childish. But whatever she did, I couldn't hate her. It is a waste of my time and I wish her the best.

In early December I left for Oslo for nine days. It was freezing up there. All the Norwegians were dumbfounded that some tourist would show up at this time of the year. But I never visit countries. I visit the people living in them. I had a great time with my friend in Oslo. I was now jobless so I decided that I would take a month off and then look for a job in the New Year.

I had a great time drinking wine and chatting to my friend. That's all we did and we hardly left the apartment. It was a relaxing vacation with so much laughter that I was sad to leave.

12

The Metamorphosis of a Dragon

The Year 2003

"Our greatest glory
is not in never falling,
but in rising
every time we fall."
—*Confucius*

Unfortunately for me, my father had just retired and he was living in the next-door apartment. He was a great motivator at that time. He told me that I will never find a job and that I should just marry my Italian boyfriend and cook pasta for him. Every second he would ask, "How is your job hunting going? Have you found another job?" It was twenty four hour badgering on his part. I told him to leave me in peace and that I will find a job. That is exactly what I did.

On the 17th of February 2003, I started working at a five star hotel in Geneva. In the beginning months I didn't like it so much, but then a new group of people joined and they were just like me. They were international people. I really enjoyed working there. My bosses were good to me and they never yelled at me. They were also happy with my work. If I made a mistake, they would tell me. A lot of people didn't like working there, but I did. I always asked for the 3 p.m. to midnight shift. A group of us would always go out after work.

In May, my boyfriend and I broke up, he wanted marriage and I didn't love him enough. It was a shame, because he was a nice person. There was nothing fundamentally wrong with him. After him I slowly fell in love with another man. We had a short-lived affair because in October things started to change. But I really liked him. I also knew this relationship was going nowhere.

The night before the Robbie Williams concert, I told my friend that we were going to the concert. She looked at me like I was crazy since we didn't have any tickets. I just told her to calm down and that we are going. At the concert I bought three tickets for five hundred Swiss Francs from a scalper, something I would never do. My friends were stunned, but happy. They ran right into the centre of the concert while I stayed on the side. At the end of the concert, it seemed like we were at two different concerts. Mainly because I was in a mania and Robbie Williams was singing subliminal messages to me.

I thought that I could control being in a mania, but then it controlled me. Just thinking I could control this mania, is like having the audacity of stepping into a ring of lions and tigers at a circus without any training.

One evening I was working at the reception in the hotel and there was this awful floral arrangement that looked like a scarecrow. It was the ugliest thing in the world. It also look liked a crucifix. Who could have the bad taste of putting that in a hotel with an international clientele? I felt that this thing was sending me evil vibes, so in matter of 2 seconds I kicked it over and returned to the front desk as if nothing happened. Later a hotel guest even congratulated me for doing this, because he too was not impressed with the lobby decor.

In a reception briefing I threw an empty soda can at another girl. This mania was different; it was a violent mania. Of course I was fired on the spot and I don't blame them. I would have fired myself.

I believe this mania was violent, because I had swallowed everything that had happened to me over the years and simply laughed it off. I didn't take what happened to me seriously enough and throughout all the difficult episodes I had put on a brave face to make the environment around me more pleasant. I didn't want the people around me to suffer, even though I was suffering the most.

All the insults, all the pain and all the injustice that I saw brought out a rage that I never felt or even dared to express before. I think I saw too much too soon and experienced too many things in too short a time span. So the sleeping dragon in me woke up and unleashed herself. The dragon had been provoked too many times. Funnily enough I was born in the year of dragon. But I can't justify my actions to the Chinese horoscope.

Another night I met a guy and I went back to his hotel room with him. I completely trashed the room. After that I knew I had passed all the boundaries of sanity. This was so out of character. Later that night I went to a very expensive night club. It was deserted with only the beautiful Russian prostitutes. I sat down and ordered a drink. They came to sit with me, because they had nothing else to do. I ordered drinks for everyone and charged it on my credit card. We kept drinking and laughing until the bouncer came to inform me that there was no credit left. I told him he was a liar and started punching him. Then the manager came and brought me into some weird room that looked liked a vampire's boardroom.

Finally the cops came, I started fighting and insulting them. This cop didn't even bother to reason with me he just pinned me to the floor and handcuffed me. In the car he sat next to me, that's when I noticed that he was really handsome. I told him in French, "You are really handsome." He didn't react because he knew I was crazy.

At the police station my psychiatrist came to pick me up. She took me to the state mental hospital. When I arrived, they locked me up in a room with a mattress on the floor and gave me an injection to sedate me. The next day I asked the nurse for cigarettes. She came every thirty minutes with a cigarette. My cigarette packet had a proper medical label on it. I was then transferred to the hospital in Geneva, which was closer to my house.

The psychiatric ward in the Geneva hospital was half a floor, but luckily I had my own room. It was really boring there. There was only a T.V room. The first night there I decided to escape. I called the nurse. As soon as she opened the door I ran and took a bus into town. Then I took a taxi back to the nightclub, when I arrived the bar tender said I could only come in if I drank non alcoholic beverages. I also apologized to the bouncer for hitting him. I again invited all the Russian prostitutes for champagne (CHF six hundred), because otherwise they couldn't sit with me. I also wanted to save them from having to sell their bodies.

I was having a great time when two people showed up out of nowhere. They asked if I was Livia Moser. I said, "Yes" and then they told me they were the criminal police and that they were here to bring me back to the hospital. These two cops were not in uniform. They drove me back and I didn't try to escape again. I guess I had to earn my departure. So it was back to being 'Miss Well Behaved.'

The people in the ward weren't that interesting except for one lady. She would shout like a lunatic. Mostly she had rages because the Holy Spirit wouldn't marry her. Sometimes she made herself beautiful so that the Holy Spirit would marry her. Everyone thought she was really crazy, but I didn't. Maybe she saw things that I didn't see. It was the same thing with me; I would do and see things that others didn't understand.

The shrinks told me that I have the same illness as Winston Churchill and Napoleon. They were lucky because they lived in a time when they were no shrinks around. It's amazing how many students worldwide study these two historical figures and hail them as geniuses when they were out of their minds. Because only when you are out of your mind can you come up with such ideas.

After a while I was getting really bored. Finally they granted me permission to leave the hospital after breakfast and come back before dinner. I was happy about this. I had my own apartment then, so I could relax in my familiar surroundings. It was also possible to see friends.

I was released on the first of December, 2004. I had

spent a month there. I was not happy though. The head psychiatrist informed me that I couldn't ever go back to working in the hotel business. This news deeply saddened me. What was I going to do now? Also I had to battle with the insurance company for my monthly salary. I was sick after all. I hate insurance companies, they can cash in easily, but when it comes to paying up they are nowhere to be seen.

So here I was more drugged up than ever, with the highest dose ever and I had to call and call these bureaucrats. I am sure that they cared more about their coffee breaks than me. That pissed me off, because they were the healthy ones and they should be helping the sick. I solved my anger by having a cigarette and a cup of coffee. That always solves everything for me. So after two months I finally got paid. But it is still unforgivable.

Luckily in mid December a good friend of mine came to visit me from the States. She managed to cheer me up and I could forget about the future for a while and just enjoy the present. It was also the holiday season and that always puts me in a good mood.

I was also visiting a new shrink every month. She was quite cold in the beginning, but it got better.

13

Getting off the Roller Coaster

The Year 2004

"To be tested is good.
The challenged life
may be the best therapist."

—*Gail Sheehy*

It is difficult to write about 2004, because I don't remember much. I went to see my new shrink twice a week and the television program was my agenda. Other people had filo faxes. I was getting money from the insurance company every month so that I could live.

Most of 2004, I wasn't living, but simply existed. I felt half dead inside and just wanted someone or anything to save me. I listened to the song *"Bring me to Life"* by Evanescence over and over again. I could relate to it so much it was almost a therapy for me.

I remember that I hadn't paid my health insurance bill on time and they threatened to terminate my contract, of course they would have loved to do that. I cost them a lot of money and they would have loved to get rid of me. What angered me the most was that my insurance company knew that no other insurance company would accept me, because I am a high risk customer. It is also Swiss law to have a health insurance, so how did any of this make sense???? What complete assholes!

The insurance company's psychiatrist summoned me for an evaluation.

I went to his office that was as big as a living room with designer chairs and I told him my whole story. He thought that I could work in hotels, though other psychiatrists thought I couldn't. He also thought that I could work 100%, because he didn't think the past events of my life were anything serious at all. He basically treated me as if I had only broken a fingernail.

I got a kind letter from the insurance company, telling me that they will pay me for two more months and then I can basically take care of myself. So I am still sick, under psychiatric supervision, not working and they cut me off. If I didn't have a family, I would have been homeless with a German shepherd given to me by the government to keep me company. So now I was 28 and broke. The saddest part was that they cut me off right before December leaving me with no money to buy Christmas presents and I love buying gifts for people. Didn't they have a heart? They all had beautiful offices with designer chairs, but couldn't give money to a sick woman for December. Well Merry Christmas to you too Scrooge.

Now I know why there is such a high suicide rate in Switzerland. Because they treat the sick people like absolute garbage. Switzerland is so beautiful and so clean; it is as if the Swiss are trying to hide something. I was unlucky enough to discover Switzerland's awful secret.

If it doesn't fit get rid off it, just like all those weeds that are removed to make the countryside look beautiful. No one talks about it though. The Swiss believe they have freedom, but they don't. Everything is so controlled that if you step out of line, the system will drive you to suicide. So we all continue to live in our boxes and like hamsters spinning the wheel going nowhere. But as long as it looks good don't rock the boat.

There are so many miserable Swiss out there, but no one speaks about it, because that would not be achieving and this is an achievement-oriented country. It is by far not a soul-oriented country. The state of the soul is not at all relevant compared to the bank account.

I wasn't getting any financial support from the government. I couldn't work so I had no income. It would have been really easy and dishonest to check myself into a mental hospital for life. This would have cost my health insurance a lot of money. Luckily my family rose to the occasion and supported me financially.

There was no other alternative, but to look for a job again. I couldn't look for just any job; it had to be a stress free job, because stress as the psychiatrist said could lead to a manic outburst. Unfortunately for me there is no such thing as a stress free job. Ironically I was diagnosed as insane and illogical, but where was the logic in all of these sane, respected and specialized people's thinking.

I decided to look for a job, because I had to earn an income. If no one was going to help me, I might as well do the logical thing and look for a job, even though there was stress involved, it was my only option.

The reference from the Hotel wasn't great. It's strange that two acts of madness can erase all the hard work I had done in that hotel and that all the future employers will look at that sole piece of paper and judge me by that. I finally found a job after four months.

What I did achieve, however, is that I obtained a licence to own or run a food and beverage establishment or a hotel in the State of Geneva. I was proud that I passed that exam, because it was in French and it was in law. The problem is that I didn't have the money or the motivation to open an establishment.

Everything that I took for granted before has been taken from me; my health, my mental health and working in hotels ever again. I don't have a boyfriend and I am not looking for one. I still have my dream and that is to have my hotel, the path has just been changed. But as all roads lead to Rome, so can all roads lead to my dream.

In my mania, I have seen what heaven could be like, but I don't want to see heaven anymore. It causes too many problems, not only for me, but also for my family and friends. I will see heaven when I am dead. I am also weary of the future because I think the worst is yet to come. Could this really be the end of the ride? I hope so; let me go to the carousel for a while.

Even though these past ten years have been like a roller coaster, they have also been like a carousel. I noticed that the same events happened over and over again. I was going around in circles. Actually I was in an amusement park. I had been in the hall of mirrors, in the torture chamber, the haunted house and the bumper cars.

I felt like I was stuck in an amusement park and I couldn't get out no matter how hard I tried. Then I realized that I was holding myself captive and no one else. If I wanted to leave I had to change. I had to learn where the holes were in the fun house, so I wouldn't fall through them again.

I also realized that I was a bit like a phoenix; I would fly high, crash and burn and then rise again from the ashes. The older I get, the more painful the memories are. While I was writing this book I almost cried at some parts, laughed at others.

What I don't understand is that most of the world is waiting for the second coming. But if anyone says I am the Son of God, I am the life and the way, follow me and you shall be saved, they will clearly end up in the mental hospital for grand delusions. So I suggest people stop waiting for the saviour and go save themselves! If, however, you are looking for a second Jesus check your closest mental hospital.

I did do something positive in the year 2004; I went to Spain to visit my good friend for ten days and it was a ball. The days were filled with laughter, good food and there was even a summer romance involved. I felt like I was in some cheap novel.

Though I enjoyed myself in Spain, I was looking forward to going back home. Home was now, finally, Switzerland. I had my routine and my friends there and it was where I wanted to live.

I stepped out of the airport into the warm sunshine of Geneva, Switzerland. I was so relieved to be back in Switzerland because I loved the country so much, it had saved my life, and turned me into a woman I can admire today. I had had a tough decade behind me.

> "Some men see things as they are
> and ask why.
> Others dream things that never were
> and ask why not."
>
> —*George Bernard Shaw*

I am sure that you all wanted a happy ending. You probably wanted to hear that I am married living in a house with a white picket fence, a golden retriever and 2.5 children. But I don't. I have a better ending for you, I am still alive and that in itself is a miracle. I made it with my personality intact, just wiser. Unfortunately I won't get any medals for this, so I thought I would write a book and share my story to get some prize, just kidding.

I am only 28 and have my whole life in front of

me. What I still do have is my sense of humour. If I lose that, then I will call it a day. But now there is no other choice than to fight. Sometimes I feel like I am in a baseball diamond and balls are thrown from every direction and I have to swing away at every ball that comes. If they say when life throws you lemons make lemonade, I would have a lot of lemonade.

Mental illness is hard to accept and I admire and respect all the people who were in mental hospitals. Believe only in yourself, because it is you that you have to live with 24/7. It isn't the end of the world. I too asked God to take my soul a number of times. I am not going to kill myself, because that would be like quitting.

For all the people that were never in mental hospitals, it is not as bad as you think. The media never shows the kindness and compassion that exists in a mental hospital. I don't recommend you go there nor am I suggesting you go.

It does leave me with a question that is difficult to answer, which world is more real. The outside world where everyone wears masks? Or the mental hospital where no one wears a mask?

Who has the right to give a 16-year-old boy a label that he has to wear for the rest of his life? Is he crazy because he could write Chinese figures at the age of two? He even looked like Bruce Lee, can't he be Bruce Lee reincarnated? Look at the Dalai Lama. He is hailed throughout the world and yet believes he has been reincarnated over and over again as do all his people. So what is the fundamental difference?

Who has the right to tell you that you may as well give up because you are bipolar? No one, actually there is someone and that is only yourself. You can either listen or take the label seriously.

I am not just bipolar; I am thousands of many things as well. I am a brunette, how is that for a label? So if society scratches off people for one label isn't that indirect mental cleaning.

Why not send all us crazies to an island and keep us there so we would not frighten society. We frighten society because we don't follow the rules and we live by our own truths.

How many of you have faced your own truths? Fought for what you thought was right, suffered injustice from some asshole with a small prick? Or an insecure female in power?

So finally, I salute the crazies of this world, embrace your craziness. It is a gift and not a curse. Being "crazy" is nothing to be ashamed of because it broadens your horizons even though a lot of suffering is involved. For the rest of you, madness lies in all of us, how can it not, because sanity is a great thing to hide behind.

All my love,

Livia

Afterword

"All of the animals
except for man
know that the principle business of life
is to enjoy it."
—*Samuel Butler*

I started writing this book in 2004 and in 2006 I continued writing it. I wrote this book not for pity, but because it is a story that must be told. I am now waiting for 100% disability insurance, because doctors have said that I can't work. I am currently battling to get this insurance. I am a Swiss citizen and it is my right to have this insurance. If they deny me the insurance, I will go for an appeal.

I realized that if I didn't call them, they wouldn't help me. At the moment my parents are financially supporting me. My friends are still the same ones that I have always had. They have been through thick and thin with me.

I am studying psychology in a University. I am studying psychology to better understand myself and to bring hope to mentally ill people. Something I wish a psychiatrist and therapist would have given me. Studying also keeps my mind off the current unfair situation.

Every week I see a psychiatrist who has helped me immensely; after all these years I found a great psychiatrist. She saved me from falling into a mania in September 2006 because of all the accumulated stress. I am sure that this mania would have ruined everything I had built up in University and I would never have been able to graduate or even worse it could have been the end of me.

The reasons I survived was because of external and internal factors. The external factors are my family and friends. The internal factors are my will to live, my humour and hope. Also I never leave a movie without finishing it, so there is no way I am going to quit in the middle of my life. I am too curious to see how the rest of my life unfolds.

Due to my mental illness society has thrown me out many times, and put me away. Now I can see that many members of society are sleepwalking unaware of the true beauty and small miracles that go on all the time. I am no longer ashamed of being "bipolar", because I want to be in this world, but never of it.

I have come full circle, I am '18 again' and I am in a university, just being a student and enjoying life. This decade (the 30's) is going to be a different decade, because I now know all the early signs of all my illness, both the kidney and the mental illness, which are vital tools.

All the other inherent survival tools have worked so far so I am optimistic of the future. I know that other challenges will arise, but without challenges, life would not only be boring but I wouldn't learn anything from the life experience only surviving a challenge provides.

Though I loved Switzerland, Switzerland didn't love me. I feel like I am in a dead end marriage where I am giving and getting nothing in return. No other country in the world had treated me as badly as my own. It's heartbreaking and disappointing. Many times have I just wanted to leave Switzerland, but I have realized that the grass isn't greener on the other side and changing my circumstances is up to me. Now I am able to see the positive and the negative qualities of Switzerland just like they exist in every country of the world. I can't blame Switzerland, or any other country or anyone for my life, the only thing I can do is look inside myself on how to improve my own life.

This reminds me of a quote that I heard a long time ago. "Sometimes it takes greater courage to stay than to leave." My addition to that quote is that I have to find the courage in myself to stay grounded and not to leave into a mania.

So, on this final note I leave you with the perfect song *"Welcome to my Truth"* by Anastacia.

Sentimental days
In a misty clouded haze
Of a memory that now feels untrue
I used to feel disguised
Now I leave the mask behind
Painting pictures that aren't so blue
The pages I've turned are the lessons I've learned

[Chorus:]
Somebody bring up the lights I want you to see
(Don't You Feel Sorry For Me)
My life turned around
But I'm still living my dreams
(Yes it's true I've been)
I've been through it all
Hit about a million walls
Welcome to my truth.. I still love
Welcome to my truth. I still love

Tangled in a web
With a pain hard to forget
That was a time that I've now put to rest
Oh, the pages I've turned are the lessons I've learned

[Chorus]
Sentimental days
In a mist of clouded haze
Of a memory that now feels untrue

The River that was Damned

A river ran her path through the valley
Happy and wild, unashamed the river ran
Then one day a dam stopped the river
The river didn't yield
Tried to break loose
The dam was stronger
The river diverted it ran into unknown territory
Controlled and angry it rushed through foreign places
Stream and brooks emerged
Then the river understood
For the diversion had given the river opportunities
To nourish the earth that needed the river
Flowers grew
Fruits ripened
The river took the tears away
Received a lot of dirt
Saw lovers pass by
And now the river joyfully waits for whatever dam lies ahead
For a dam is no longer an obstruction, but a new chance

—Livia Moser

Intensity

I'm a person either seen as a clown, comedian or joker
No one ever took me seriously
They thought I was all a joke
They didn't see my intense side
I didn't want to let them see that side
It was MINE and Mine alone
It was too vulnerable and too precious
This was the side that thought about the universe
And questioned human emotions
The side that wondered what death was like

No one ever took me seriously

I covered my weakness with my jokes
The tears with my laughter
I walked around playing on a lie
I had hidden this side for so long

18 years to be exact
I was open and friendly
People thought they knew me
But did they?
And until now no one will ever know
No one took me seriously until it was too late
Now this poem speaks for me

—Livia Moser
June 1994

Amazing how a poem written 12 years ago could be so precise on the future. If only I had taken the poem seriously.

The Songs of the Roller Coaster Decade

1 Tease Me — Chaka Demus

2 Country Roads — John Denver

3 Love is All Around — Wet Wet Wet

4 Memory — from the musical Cats Andrew Lloyd Webber

5 One — Metallica

6 Hero — Mariah Carey

7 Greatest Love of All — Whitney Houston

8 Nothing Else Matters — Metallica

9 Living on a Prayer — Bon Jovi

10 Bring me to Life — Evanescence

11 Welcome to My Truth — Anastacia

After the endless phone calls to different administration offices that are supposed to help out people in my situation, I was granted 100% disability insurance on the 5th of October, 2006. It took me 12 years, but finally justice has been served.

I couldn't have done it all by myself, but with my psychiatrist and my social assistant we managed. I will always be grateful to them both.

It has been a long, hard and an enriching ride and without it this book would have never been written. I am happy to be clinically bipolar, because it is my wild card, my joker that I can use, so after a long time of thinking it was a curse it has been a blessing.

So to everyone keep on fighting for what you know you deserve, never give up no matter what the obstacles are. There are already so many obstacles imposed on us, don't be your own obstacle in your life as well.

Without the efforts of many people I wouldn't be here today.

First of all I would like to thank my mother Irene, my biggest teacher, who has always been there for me. She was an example of strength in the storm and always kept me safe. I would like to thank my father, Jack for taking me to the doctor when he saw the colour of my urine; otherwise I would have ignored it. He has shown me humour and the ability to laugh at anything. My sisters are next. Sarah for her constant support and Carmen for the simple joy she exudes in living. Thanks to all of my friends here and across the globe for never leaving me or being ashamed of me and for sharing your stories with me and your love and laughter. I am so blessed that to write all your names down it would be longer than the book.

Herzlichen Dank to my Aunt Doris Schneider who took the iniative to print manuscripts of this book to send to publishers. A huge thank you to Martin and Shiree Woolnough for helping me with the proofreading of this book and their unconditional, continual support in my life.

The doctors, surgeons, nurses, and psychiatrists (even the bad ones) thank you for saving my life. The people that were awful to me thank you for making me see what I was really made out of.

All the musicians with their beautiful songs and the actors who are so incredibly funny that made me laugh and are also bipolar.

Also to my teachers in the different international schools, The Swiss School of Hotel Management and the University of Webster thanks for believing in me throughout my life.

Thanks to the people who indirectly helped me like Margreet De Jong and Gilla Thompson with their books and e-mails to my mother.

And last, but not the least the funniest force in the universe God. You have always been there in my darkest hours and my happiest hours. My only request is that someday we can share a bottle of champagne and laugh together. You have been the gasoline in my engine when I wanted to quit and go home to you. Stay cool G.

My greatest wish to all of you is that you are simply yourselves because then you find the light in you and that's when you truly and wholy (no it isn't a typo) live.

www.ingramcontent.com/pod-product-compliance
Ingram Content Group UK Ltd.
Pitfield, Milton Keynes, MK11 3LW, UK
UKHW021053270726
13967UKWH00012B/642